NATIONALIZED
COMPANIES

NATIONALIZED COMPANIES: A THREAT TO AMERICAN BUSINESS

R. Joseph Monsen
and
Kenneth D. Walters

McGraw-Hill Book Company

New York St. Louis San Francisco Hamburg London Mexico Toronto

1 2 3 4 5 6 7 8 9 D O C D O C 8 7 6 5 4 3

ISBN 0-07-071569-6

LIBRARY OF CONGRESS CATALOGING IN PUBLICATION DATA
Monsen, R. Joseph.
Nationalized companies.
1. Government business enterprises—Europe.
I. Walters, Kenneth D. II. Title.
HD4138.M66 1983   338.94'04   82–20902
ISBN 0–07–071569–6

Book design by Sharkey Design

Elaine
and
Karla

ACKNOWLEDGMENTS

For the past six years we have been studying nationalized and state-owned companies and attempting to evaluate the pros and cons of government ownership. In the process we realized the great general interest in the topic and became persuaded to write a study that would be of interest to more than economists. For this reason we have approached the subject from a broader political, economic, and managerial perspective.

We wish to express our deep appreciation to the many government officials and nationalized company executives in Great Britain, France, Italy, West Germany, Norway, Sweden, and Austria, who gave so generously of their time and so candidly of their views. Nearly all of the scores of officials and executives we contacted were cooperative and helpful. These interviews enabled us to understand financial reports of the European nationalized companies which might have been otherwise inscrutable. We have, as well, benefited greatly from the work of other European and American scholars studying state-owned firms and from countless government studies and official reports. Also, we wish to thank the Camargo Foundation in Cassis, France for providing an unusually pleasant library and premises where parts of the book were written. Finally, we wish to express our gratitude to Mrs. Brigid King for her valued secretarial help.

CONTENTS

INTRODUCTION

Capitalism in Western Europe is changing rapidly. In some countries state-owned companies amount to nearly half of the industrial sector, including control of key industries. European governments now have a direct ownership stake in over half of Europe's fifty largest companies. Few Americans are aware that many familiar companies are government owned. Renault, Alfa Romeo, British Petroleum, Airbus Consortium, British Leyland, Volkswagen, Swedish Steel, and Rolls-Royce—to name only a few—are companies in which governments are the sole or largest shareholder. Government companies in Western Europe make aluminum pans, airplane engines, tractors, computer software, cakes, office equipment, advanced electronic equipment, computers, and cars and trucks—and run hotel chains. Although the private sector is for the moment still larger than the state-owned sector, the state-owned segment is beginning to dominate in more and more industries, and it expands to new products and markets each year.

The spread of European state-owned companies has also affected the United States. Americans who once looked on nationalization as a European novelty now regard the issue more seriously, as the controversy over the Chrysler bail-out testified.

European trends have influenced American capitalism in a variety of ways: The direct purchase of United States companies by foreign state-owned enterprises (such as Sohio, Ashland Coal, Copperweld, Mack Trucks, and Texasgulf); the temptation to American politicians to have government take over, directly or indirectly, large companies in trouble; and the competitive threat that nationalized companies, because of their special advantages, represent to private companies.

Could European-style nationalization become a pattern for the United States? Although no major political party in the United States has ever made nationalization a plank in its platform, discussion of the option has increased in the past decade. John Kenneth Galbraith has urged that state ownership be considered to control large corporations.[1] A prominent labor leader, William Wimpisinger, advocates nationalization for firms that "rig prices" in transportation, petroleum, and other industries.[2] When public confidence in the oil companies dipped sharply in the 1970s, many began to urge that a federally owned oil company be set up as a yardstick to measure oil company profits and to gather independent data on U.S. oil reserves and development costs. In 1973, then-Senator Adlai Stevenson III sponsored legislation with this goal in mind.[3]

The United States has moved toward *de facto* nationalization in some areas in recent years. Passenger rail service has been nationalized. The U.S. government has guaranteed large loans for such distressed companies as Lockheed and Chrysler. Even a conservative presidential candidate like Ronald Reagan supported government loan guarantees for Chrysler, perhaps more out of pragmatism than conviction. The point is that precedents of rescuing large companies in serious financial trouble have been set. An argument often heard in Europe in the past decade—that it is cheaper for governments to rescue large companies facing closure than to pay the staggering costs of economic and social dislocation—could become more common in the United States.

When large companies face collapse, political parties of the left and right tend to agree that drastic steps, including outright state takeovers, must be considered. Much of the nationalization in Europe in the past decade occurred under right-of-center governments that felt compelled to rescue failing companies. In the economic collapse of the 1930s, many American conservatives as well as liberals favored government economic solutions. Both presidential candidates in 1980 favored federal programs to revitalize industry, involving closer cooperation among government, business, and labor. If President Reagan's program of supply-side economics is not successful in stimulating investment and increasing jobs and productivity, the United States could turn to greater government financing of business.

One major proponent of government rescues of large companies is Felix Rohatyn, the New York investment banker and chairman of the Municipal Assistance Corporation for New York City. Rohatyn proposes:

> As a first step toward reversing (U.S. industrial decline) in an equitable manner, a "Reconstruction Finance Corporation" should be created. This federally chartered and supervised entity would intervene to shore up troubled older industries by providing equity capital to failing corporations.[4]

"The idea that the United States can function while writing off basic industries to foreign competition is nonsense," Rohatyn argues.

DOES STATE OWNERSHIP MATTER?

When one talks to the managers of European state-owned and private firms and compares their annual financial reports, one quickly discovers that there are indeed differences between the behavior of state-owned Renault and privately owned Peugeot, Salzgitter and Thyssen, Alfa Romeo and Fiat. The state-owned firm differs in its purpose and objectives. Performance and results are not *less* important in the state-owned firm, but they are usually measured and defined differently.

Performance in a state-owned company means balancing a wide number of competing goals, which become important ends in themselves for judging the company's performance. The government as owner is interested in whether the company contributed to the nation's export drive, whether it managed to avoid laying off employees, and whether it kept domestic consumer prices under control. One rarely hears about a state-owned company's return on investment, its return on capital, or on the profitability of its assets.

When a business enterprise is owned by the government, the purpose of nationalization becomes the focal point for a debate about the policies that should be pursued by the firm. In fact, there appears to be no more ponderously debated topic in European politics than the question: What goal or mixture of goals should state firms pursue? There are two schools of thought (one could say two ideologies) on this question. The "hard line" urges that clear and precise performance criteria, mostly economic, should be used to measure the performance of state-owned firms. This school stresses that profits are the best single measure of efficiency, even for state-owned firms, since profit is nothing more than the difference between revenues and costs. Privately owned firms are principally interested in their profitability. Without profits they cannot retain and attract capital and eventually must close up shop. Whatever the oversimplifications of the economic theorem that companies seek to maximize their profits, there remains a basic truth that profitability is necessary for long-term survival for the private firm. Some believe the same test should apply to state-owned companies. If a state-owned company cannot return profits to its owners—the taxpayers and citizens—it deserves to go out of business rather than be subsidized indefinitely.

The view that profits should be the major goal of the state-owned firm, whatever its logic, has not received wide support from citizens and governments; so state-owned firms have not generally been held to this test. It is hard to explain to workers and consumers the function of profits in measuring efficiency—especially when people link profits with capitalism. Sir Peter Parker, chairman of British Rail, did not begin to realize how hard a task he had undertaken when he stated that he wanted to "deodorize profits."

The other school of thought, the "soft line," advocates different performance criteria for state-owned firms. Companies and managers, in this view, should be judged on how well they have increased employment, kept prices down, contributed to exports, or developed new technology. Multiple goals require that priorities be established to give managers guidance as to what matters deserve the greatest resources and attention. Should social goals take precedence over profits? If profits are not earned, investment must be financed from external sources, often to the detriment of private business.

The persistence of the debate between the hard-line and soft-line schools suggests that the choice of the state firms' goals is as fundamental as the question of whether to have state-owned firms in the first place. The answer to both questions may depend fundamentally on ideological predispositions.

THE APPEAL OF NATIONALIZATION

What is the appeal of nationalization? Few nationalized companies perform as well as privately owned ones. We have located three possible explanations. First, socialists do not necessarily make decisions on the basis of the same data as capitalists do. Second, the need to win elections frequently converts even conservative politicians faced with the prospects of high unemployment caused by companies in trouble. Thus democracy puts a premium on short-run economic solutions, like nationalization, that may gain votes. Third, state ownership as a means of revamping and insulating domestic industries has become popular with governments seeking to balance their trade deficits and protect national markets.

How can nationalized companies simultaneously be both economic failures and competitive threats? As we argue, most nationalized companies (with the exception of oil) have seldom done more than break even over the past decade, and most have lost money. Compared to the performance of private companies state-owned companies have had a poor financial record. Yet because they have special advantages from the government, they are often able to undercut private companies, nationally and internationally.

The growth of public-owned companies, coupled with their tendency to perform less well than the private sector, does not bode well for Western Europe's long-range growth or standard of living. Politicians in Western Europe have failed to explain satisfactorily their governments' behavior in nationalizing more and more private companies. Ideology and nationalism are prominent in such non-explanations.

Our study and research focused on state-owned* firms in Western Europe, although occasionally we do refer to firms in other democratic developed economies such as Japan. We did not examine the state firms of the developing countries in this study.

The aim of this book is to explain the forces behind the rapid rise of nationalized companies, how they differ from private firms, and how their operations create serious problems both for their countries' domestic economics and for privately owned companies. The implications for the world business community are critical.

---

* In this book we use the terms "state-owned firms," "state firms," and "nationalized firms" interchangeably, although we recognize that some may draw distinctions based on whether a firm was at one time privately owned.

CHAPTER ONE

THE SPREADING NATIONALIZATION OF EUROPEAN INDUSTRY

State-owned firms are not new to Europe. Nationalized companies have dominated in the public utilities of transportation, electricity, telephone service, and natural gas for decades. State monopolies in the production and sale of tobacco, alcohol, and salt have also been common, primarily to raise revenues for the government. "Accidental" state firms—such as Charles de Gaulle's nationalization of Renault as punishment for its cooperation with Nazi Germany—were notable as exceptions.

As recently as 1970 not a single manufacturing industry in which state-owned firms held an important share of industrial output could be found in Western Europe. That has now changed radically. In a number of industries, state-owned firms have gained a dominant, or significant, position in European markets. The list includes some of the most important industrial sectors, including aerospace, steel, aluminum, shipbuilding, and automobiles.

Today state-owned firms can be found in virtually all industries in Europe. New state firms in the 1970s were created or nationalized in pharmaceuticals, electronics, computers, office equipment, oil, microelectronics, chemicals, petrochemicals, pulp and paper, and telecommunications. Each year more firms are drawn into the state-owned sector. In addition, many state-owned firms have embarked on a strategy for international expansion and diversification. Now many of the top foreign multinationals are owned and controlled by their governments.

How can we account for the increase in state ownership in the major Western European countries? To understand the nationalization trends in Europe, it will be helpful first to examine what has occurred in several countries. France, with the recent election of a

1

Socialist-Communist government, which has generated considerable world-wide attention, is an excellent place to begin.

FRANCE

The substantial increase in state ownership of industrial firms in France throughout the 1970s was temporarily overshadowed by the 1981 election of the socialist-communist government. That coalition since 1972 had offered France a "common program" to nationalize the core of the French industrial economy. On the nationalization issue, François Mitterrand's socialism resembles more the left wing of Britain's Labour party than West Germany's Social Democratic party, headed by Helmut Schmidt. Especially on nationalization, Mitterrand placed himself on the left of the French Socialist party—with the Marxist position. According to the ousted President Valery Giscard d'Estaing, Mitterrand will in time bring one-half of French industry under state ownership.

In the election program of the French Socialist party, the list of firms to be nationalized was extensive. The government brought into the state's hands thirty-six banks, essentially those banks which escaped the postwar state takeovers. Only foreign banks and small French banks were excluded. Such bankers as Baron Guy de Rothschild complained bitterly that not only banks themselves, but their industrial holdings as well, were nationalized. Included in the list of banks were Suez and Paribas, two big bank holding companies which, along with the state's existing holdings, had formed a triumvirate of shareholding power in France. Nationalization of Suez and Paribas included both their industrial and foreign holdings; bold private takeover bids for Paribas Suisse and Cobepa snatched from the state's hands some of Paribas foreign interests.

Also nationalized were many of the top French industrial firms. CGE is France's largest electrical, electronics, and nuclear engineering group and the third largest European concern in the field. Its subsidiary, CIT-Alcatel, is France's telecommunications specialist. St.-Gobain, France's leading building materials manufacturer (glass, iron pipe, insulation materials) recently diversified into high technology industries; it also holds a 30 percent stake in Olivetti. Pechiney-Ugine, Kuhlmann, the aluminum, steel, and chemicals firm, has the biggest foothold in the United States through its subsidiary, Pucko. Rhône-Poulenc, traditionally the largest company in the French chemicals industry, has been expanding into processed chemicals, animal food additives, engineering plastics, and silicones. Thomson-Brandt, the electrical, electronics, appliances, and arms manufacturer, included over 100 subsidiaries, with thirty production plants outside of France. The government also fully nationalized Dassault, the aircraft manufacturer, and has taken a 51 percent stake in Matra, the missiles, guidance, watches, and electronics group. Also on the Socialist party's list of firms to nationalize was: CII-Honeywell Bull, the computer firm established, heavily financed by the French government, and already controlled by St.-Gobain; ITT-France; and Roussal-Uclaf, the pharmaceuticals firm that is a subsidiary of Hoechst, the West German company. The Socialist party has also promised to raise the state's holdings in France's two major oil companies and take a minority stake in Peugeot, although no action has yet been taken on these.

The sheer scope of nationalization certainly rendered the French economy among the most collectivized in Western Europe. In the election campaign leading to the socialists' large victory, the socialist party rejected the comparison with nationalizations in Great Britain, saying that the French plan was to nationalize companies that were doing well, not the "lame ducks." Mitterrand has also said that nationalization of industry was necessary in a nation the size of France where "monopolies exist in the the hands of a family or company." If such monopolies involve "key economic interests," the state should own them, he told James Reston of *The New York Times* after his election victory. In sum, the French socialist government's philosophy on the state ownership issue is what Lenin called the "commanding heights" of the economy should be state-owned.

Even before the election of the socialist government in 1981, state ownership of industry had been rapidly increasing during the 1970s. The single largest expansion of state ownership was the government's gigantic rescue of the two largest French steel companies, Usinor and Sacilor, in 1978. Many other rescues of private companies, often by state-owned firms, also occurred. Renault's acquisition and rebuilding of Berliet, Citroën's ailing truck subsidiary, is an excellent example.

The central trend underlying French nationalization in the 1970s was the energetic expansion and diversification of existing state-owned companies into new product markets and new countries. From a political point of view, internal growth and diversification are less visible and, therefore, less controversial ways of expanding state ownership in France. Edouard Bonnefous, as president of the French senate's finance commission, traced the process of what he called the "creeping nationalization" of French industry via diversification. He points out that, while the number of French state-owned companies actually declined from 170 to 130, their subsidiaries multiplied from 266 to 650. The Bonnefous study traces the tremendous growth of subsidiaries of the major French state-owned companies, especially Elf-Aquitaine, Renault, and Air France.[1]

It is also significant that French state-owned banks not only facilitated this expansion, but were themselves among the fastest growing enterprises in the world. The largest single expansion of French banks abroad was Banque Nationale de Paris' purchase of Bank of the West in California. Now the top four French banks are listed among the ten largest banks in the world, a claim that neither the United States, Britain, nor Japan can make.

The most dramatic expansion was Renault's recent thrust into the United States by purchasing a large stake in Mack Trucks, and a few months later, buying a controlling block of stock in American Motors. This gives Renault a ready-made dealer network in the United States, in addition to existing factories which are now manufacturing Renault automobiles. Renault continues to push ahead with an optimistic and aggressive policy of international investment, as in its takeover of car rental companies in Europe. Renault's recent stake in Volvo Car in the Netherlands (a subsidiary of the Swedish parent company), coupled with numerous investments in other nations, show that the firm is now a major multinational. It has diversified into numerous industries throughout the world, such as agricultural machinery, trucks, machine tools, robotics, and agricultural products. Renault's subsidiaries are rapidly expanding in Austria, Mexico, Portugal, Spain, Romania, and the United States.

A vigorous program of international expansion has also been conducted by Elf-Aquitaine, the state oil company. In recent years, Elf has used its oil profits to diversify, especially in France and the United States, culminating with Elf's purchase of Texasgulf, the U.S. natural resources giant—the largest acquisition ever made by a French company. Other recent Elf acquisitions and diversification include interests in chemicals, biotechnology, pharmaceuticals, metals, plastics, and solar energy. Another example of its U.S. acquisitions is the purchase of M & T Chemicals, Inc., a U.S. subsidiary of American Can Co., with activities in chemical products for processing plastics, metals, textiles, and agricultural products, and in paint and electronic components. Elf's pharmaceutical subsidiary, Parcor, has itself aggressively acquired small laboratories that are expert in research—but not in finance and management. Elf also purchased Rhône-Poulenc's extensive holdings in petrochemicals and polymers. Elf's takeover attempts have become controversial. Elf has confirmed it held exploratory takeover talks with the U.S. oil company Kerr-McGee, but the French government —and perhaps the United States government—told Elf to back off. But with the Socialists in power, Elf was able to take over Texasgulf.

The French government, which historically has held 75 percent of Elf's stock, announced in 1980 that it was reducing its holdings to 51 percent. While leftists deplored this as "denationalization," more careful observers realized that the proceeds of the sale would be earmarked for further acquisitions by Elf. Thus the government kept control of Elf, while greatly increasing the total assets under its control by using the proceeds of the sale for expansion.

The French government in the 1970s was opposed to outright forced nationalizations of private business; hence, the government used state investment as a strategy to gain more control in certain lines of business, especially to increase exports and minimize imports. By encouraging large state-owned companies to diversify into high technology areas, the government strategy has been to concentrate a greater share of high technology industries in French hands. It has put huge sums of money into building a national telecommunications industry, which the government hopes will have major export potential. The goal is to support French businesses by using the resources and purchasing power of the state-owned companies. Similarly, the French government has carved out special national market interests in industrial robots, biotechnology, and office automation.

Nowhere is the French strategy clearer in the creation of new state-owned enterprises than Technip, a state-created engineering corporation owned by a consortium of mostly government-owned companies and banks. Technip is an aggressive competitor for international contracts, primarily by offering financing that includes government backed loans at low rates, export credits, and government promises of product buy-backs from the factories that it builds.

Nationalized Companies

GREAT BRITAIN

The expansion in French state ownership in the 1970s was marked by aggressive diversification into new markets at home and abroad, largely on the basis of offensive measures. The British chiefly relied on nationalization, not as an offensive economic weapon, but as a defensive one. British governments, both Conservative and Labour, felt compelled to take into state ownership firms which had a long tradition in British business, were responsible for thousands of jobs and much of the nation's exports, but were failing badly.

The decade began with the sudden financial collapse in 1971 of Rolls-Royce, one of Britain's most prestigious firms. Edward Heath's Conservative government quickly nationalized Rolls-Royce. This rescue established nationalization as a legitimate British industrial policy to save firms and jobs—a point endlessly repeated throughout the decade by Labour governments. Whenever Conservative party politicians complained about Labour's ambitious plans for more nationalization, Labour supporters gleefully reminded them, and the voters, that the precedent had been set in 1971 by the Conservative Heath government.

The nationalization of Rolls-Royce made British Leyland's rescue in 1974 somewhat easier, although the price tag for British Leyland was far higher than that of Rolls-Royce. Leyland employed 250,000 workers, was a major exporter, and represented the last major British-owned auto manufacturer. A Conservative government would almost certainly have nationalized it, had it been in power. The other major rescue was the establishment of British Shipbuilders, putting together the financially disastrous pieces of the once dominant British shipbuilding industry. Many other rescues of medium- and small-sized companies occurred as well.

Quite aside from the rescues which both major parties fundamentally supported—even as U.S. presidential candidate Ronald Reagan supported government loan guarantees for Chrysler—the political parties in Britain in the 1970s were preoccupied with the issue of nationalization, not merely at the pragmatic, but even more at the ideological, level. The Labour party's "Programme 1973" included the proposal that the top twenty or twenty-five manufacturing companies should be nationalized. The leading academic architect of the Labour party's nationalization proposals, Professor Stuart Holland, argued that "nationalization should not be used simply to salvage those firms which private enterprise has driven to the edge of bankruptcy, but to undertake transformed production for the new social bill of goods." This was the rationale for Labour party proposals to nationalize the "commanding heights" of the economy. Throughout the decade, Labour party officials and trade union leaders issued numerous calls to nationalize not only the "commanding heights," but the pharmaceutical industry, the banks, the insurance companies, the construction industry, and farmland as well. Each annual conference of the Labour party passed strongly worded resolutions, calling for substantial new nationalization.

The pro-nationalization forces had three major "ideological" victories in policies actually undertaken in the 1970s. The first was the nationalization of the aerospace companies, including Hawker-Siddeley Dynamics, Hawker-Siddeley Aviation, and British Aircraft Corporation. These firms were not only important producers of civil aircraft, but big exporters of military equipment—a profitable and fast growing business. Unlike Rolls-Royce and British Leyland, companies which had come hat in hand to the government, the aerospace companies had fiercely resisted state takeover. Such unfriendly nationalization was much more controversial than the rescues had been.

A second major victory of the left wing was the decision to establish the state-owned British National Oil Corporation to exploit North Sea oil. The political argument for setting up the company was that oil revenues should accrue to the British people, not to the oil multinationals. The Labour government wanted a state-owned company to manage the North Sea project. Upon coming to power, Margaret Thatcher had second thoughts about her 1977 promise to dismantle the British National Oil Corporation. Ironically, in view of Britain's budgetary deficits, BNOC's healthy and growing profits are just what the Thatcher government, with its severe budget balancing problems, came to love. Whether the oil revenues will be earmarked for special projects, such as industrial regeneration, is still open to debate. One branch of the Labour party would use the oil money for new nationalization, as proposed in Norway.

A third ideological victory for the left wing was the establishment of the National Enterprise Board, a state holding company which former Prime Minister Harold Wilson called "the biggest leap forward in economic thinking and policy since the war." Originally patterned after the Italian holding company, IRI, British socialists saw in the NEB the potential for establishing a large state-owned presence in the entire industrial economy, preferably with a major firm in each industry. The National Enterprise Board was given power to make competitive bids for the stock of unsuspecting private firms, in classic takeover fashion. Its initial budget was £ 1 (one) billion, not enough to control the "commanding heights" of the economy, but enough to scare some managers who at first wondered whether their major stockholder in the future would be the government. But the National Enterprise Board was mostly active in the 1970s in acquiring and helping small companies. It has had neither the financial capital nor the political capital to further the "socialization" of British industry, the dream of its enthusiastic founders.

If the National Enterprise Board did not usher in a new full blown socialism in Britain, under Labour party rule, neither did it disappear as many predicted it would if Margaret Thatcher came to power as Prime Minister. The Thatcher government has used it as a source of capital for high technology ventures that do not appear to attract sufficient capital from the private sector in Britain. This essentially continues the policy toward the NEB begun by the Callaghan government; computers, microelectronics, and other exotic technologies (the largest being Celltech, a genetic engineering company) are the priority areas for investment. Even so determined an exponent of capitalism as Thatcher has come to accept, if not openly advocate, the role of state ownership in new high technology businesses. A new company, called the British Technology Group, is the merged version of the National Enterprise Board and the National Research Development Corporation.

A major campaign promise of the Conservative party in the 1979 election was denationalization. But Prime Minister Thatcher, who seeks to roll back the tide of British socialism, has not found it feasible to give up control of the state-owned companies British Airways and British Aerospace. What was called the "sale of the century" by the press has turned out to be a sale of majority holdings in British Aerospace. The proposals to sell only up to 51 percent of British Airways, have been delayed in the case of the loss-riddled company. Margaret Thatcher has also made no secret of the fact that she would like to return such firms as British Shipbuilders, British Steel, and British Leyland to private ownership. But as of mid-1983, the Thatcher government had not yet been able to return any major British state-owned company to private sector control.

Thatcher has reduced the government's holdings in British Petroleum (from 68 percent in 1977), although the government shows no inclination to totally divest itself of BP, and thereby relinquish potential control. Meanwhile, BP has not only acquired Selection Trust for nearly $1 billion but, through its Sohio subsidiary, purchased Kennecott Corporation and a large share of U.S. Steel's coal reserves.

Great Britain ended the decade of the 1970s with a sizable list of large new state-owned companies. They represented a mixture of rescues of failing companies, high technology ventures, and nationalizations for ideological reasons.

ITALY

Italy entered the decade of the 1970s with one of the largest state-owned sectors in Europe. Its position had been created by government officials who followed a tradition established in the 1950s and 1960s—the rapid diversification by all its major state-owned holding companies. Further diversification was a natural development for a company already highly diversified. For example, IRI, the center-piece of the Italian economy, controls the Finsider steel group, Alitalia, Finnmeccanica, four major commercial banks, and scores of other enterprises. It is the prime example of the literally thousands of industrial bureaucracies which have continued to proliferate during over thirty years of Christian Democratic rule.

Recent expansions in state ownership in Italy can be broken down into two periods, the early and late 1970s. In the early 1970s, the government adopted a deliberate policy to develop a national capacity in such industries as electronics, aerospace, and nuclear energy. The major state holding companies were given funds to expand and develop in these and other high technology areas. In 1971, a state company called GEPI was set up, using public capital to assist small- and medium-size firms. By the end of 1975, it had fifty-four firms with a total of 26,000 employees. The government also set up a new state holding company for mining, mineral, and metallurgical groups, EGAM. Between 1971 and 1975, EGAM acquired over forty previously private companies in textile machinery. EGAM was later liquidated, and its assets passed on to IRI and ENI.

The sometimes curious pattern of expansion of Italian state-owned enterprises in the 1970s is shown by the purchase of major newspapers by the various state-owned conglomerates. All the major state-owned groups spent heavily to buy control of major newspapers, as well as acquiring numerous other press ventures, such as

Nationalized Companies

weekly news magazines. It is said that the state company SIR (since merged into ENI) controlled the press in Sardinia, where its major plants operated. ENI not only acquired a stake in several newspapers, but its own press agency as well.

One surprise development in the 1970s was the Communist party's criticism of state-owned enterprises. Some attribute this partly to the huge size of the Italian state-owned sector. The major state holding companies already control the largest banks, important sections of the automotive, chemicals, communications, electronics, mining and metallurgical industries. They also have holdings in food, tourism, engineering, steel, oil and energy, and other industries; so, the "commanding heights" of the economy appear to be already firmly under state ownership. But the Communists were bothered by a suspicion that the state-owned enterprises serve the personal and political purposes of the ruling Christian Democratic party. Further nationalization only put more resources in the hands of the ruling parties, and left the Communists out.

The second half of the 1970s was marked by a much more aggressive role by the state-owned banks in rescuing and even taking ownership in previously private firms. Other state companies in the 1980s are continuing to gobble up small firms. Aeritalia, the state aircraft manufacturer, took over two companies in 1981 and has its eyes on still others. But the state's minority stake in Montedison, the chemicals giant, was sold to the private sector in 1981.

The new role of the state-owned banks as shareholders and major rescuers raises new questions about the extent to which many of these large companies can still be accurately considered to be privately owned. Mediobanca rescued the Pirelli tires and cable firm where a consortium of mostly state-owned banks was to acquire a 24 percent shareholding in the company. Similar operations have been undertaken for other previously private companies, such as Olivetti and Montefibre. Some have even speculated that if Fiat continues on its present downward course, it could eventually end up among Italy's state-owned conglomerates. It is now estimated that the public sector accounts for about 65 percent of all credit extended by the banking system—a dramatic statistic indicating the extent to which Italy's industrial future is primarily channeled through government-owned companies.

The extremely shaky credit of the large state-owned conglomerates reached crisis proportions in the late 1970s, and the government has increasingly asked the state-owned banks to take a larger role in rescuing failing state firms. Consortia of the mainly state-owned banks formulated rescue programs for two major chemical groups. The state banks have protested about being burdened with the cost of rescues of companies in trouble, yet the new chairmen of the banks are beholden to political interests for their jobs and find it difficult to refuse requests that they grant credit, not on the basis of a business judgment, but on political grounds. Credit Italiano, Banco Commerciale Italiana, and Banco di Roma, the three big banks controlled by IRI, are all examples.

WEST GERMANY

Few governments in Western Europe appear, on the face of it, to be as fundamentally opposed to new nationalization as the Federal German Government (West Germany). Nationalization has rarely been a political issue in the national elections. The Social Democrats and the Free Democrats see almost eye to eye with the Christian Democratic party on the need for maintaining Germany as a private enterprise economy. Labor unions' calls to nationalize troubled companies have thus far fallen on deaf ears.

Yet the German government has very large investments in industry, often shared with private shareholders. VEBA, West Germany's largest industrial company, is 44 percent state-owned. With the private shares spread widely, the government is easily able to control the firm. Volkswagen, the auto giant, is still 40 percent government-owned, with half of government's stake in the hands of the state government of Lower Saxony, although the government divested itself of majority ownership in 1961. Vereinigte Industrie Unternehmungen (VIAG) is another state-owned conglomerate with interests in aluminum, steel, shipbuilding. Salzgitter is a state-owned engineering, steel, shipbuilding, oil and gas concern. Saarbergwerke specializes in power plants. Figures published by the German Finance Ministry show that the federal government owns holdings in up to 600 companies.

The single most important recent increase in state ownership came on the heels of the oil crisis in 1973, when West Germany realized that it had no national oil interests. As a result, VEBA and the private firm Gelsenberg were merged to create a large state-controlled group, equal in refining capacity to the largest foreign-owned company in Germany. VEBA has since expanded into a vast network of interests that now cover aluminum, petrochemicals, and glass manufacturing.

West German policy toward state ownership is different from that of countries discussed earlier. It did not blatantly "nationalize" major companies; rather, its policy was to allow and encourage large state firms to diversify into new sectors. Germany's Monopolies Commission found in 1976 that the government was the most important shareholder in the top 100 companies in Germany. Set up to defend competition and fight industrial concentration, the Monopolies Commission was highly critical of the diversification policies of the large state-owned enterprises, claiming that "the sucking up of smaller companies on the edge of their areas of operations" had become the state-owned companies' "longterm corporate strategy."

One example of the diversification of the German state-owned giants was the purchase of an oil company in the United States, Creslenn (Dallas). Volkswagen undertook an aggressive diversification program both inside and outside its traditional areas of product expertise. Its expansion in the United States made it the fourth largest domestic U.S. auto manufacturer. It purchased Chrysler's manufacturing operations in Brazil, as well as making major expansions in Mexico. Its latest move is a number of acquisitions in the office automation industry and computer systems, an area in which West Germany has lagged and where new technologies will create large markets in the future. Consistent with its status as a state-owned company that places growth ahead of profits, an executive with Triumph Adler, since 1980 a VW subsidiary, revealed that Volkswagen does not even expect any return on its investment until the end of the 1980s. Even Salzgitter, the perennial loss-making steel and engineering state-owned firm, found the cash to expand into the automotive parts business with its acquisition of a large share of Sachs AG. In 1981, loss-prone Saarbergwerke purchased 25 percent of Ashland Coal Company, one of the largest coal companies in the United States. Rheinbraun, a subsidiary of RWE, West Germany's largest power utility, acquired a 24 percent interest in coal reserves in Pennsylvania held by Consolidated Coal, a DuPont subsidiary.

NORWAY

Nationalization of industry in Norway during the 1970s set a pace that was unmatched by any other Western European nation, with

The Spreading Nationalization of European Industry

the possible exception of Portugal. The decade began with the discovery of North Sea oil, and with the almost immediate establishment of Statoil, the Norwegian state oil company that has grown, during the past ten years, to the status of a major international producer.

Norway's Labor government had early intentions of using revenue from its new oil industry to socialize much of the nation's economy. It wasted no time in buying control of Norsk Hydro through secret purchases (it already had a minority stake). The announced purpose of the takeover was to facilitate the development of a vertically integrated state petrochemical industry, with Norsk Hydro under the same ownership as the state oil company. State banks steadily expanded during the Labor rule of the 1970s as well. There are now eight of them, providing cheap loans for a variety of special purposes. In 1974, the government bought one-half of Alcan Aluminum's 50 percent holding in Aardal og Sundal Verk, increasing state ownership in the firm to 75 percent. Five years later Alcan, believing ASV should expand its primary metal capacity, sold the government the rest of its ASV holdings, protesting the government's policy of diversifying into aluminum fabrication.

In 1975, the state bought British Petroleum's ownership stake in a "downstream" oil company, NNB, which held a refinery and a chain of depots, sales facilities, a tanker, and 1000 gasoline stations. This, coupled with further state takeovers in petroleum, effectively achieved a state dominated marketing organization in oil.

In 1977, the state rescued Tandberg, the electronics firm—a rescue that became a bankruptcy when the state cash transfusion did not stop Tandberg's cash hemorrhaging.

In 1978, the Norwegian government attempted to take a 40 percent stake in the Swedish automaker Volvo, becoming the largest stockholder, but Volvo's shareholders blocked the deal. Norsk Hydro continued to expand its international operations, purchasing Vinatex, the third largest producer of polyvinyl chloride in Great Britain. Further acquisitions were fertilizer companies in Belgium, Great Britain, and Sweden, as Norsk Hydro attempted to strengthen its position as an international manufacturer of fertilizer. Norsk Hydro, now the largest industrial company in Norway, established a new U.S. company, Norsk Hydro Aluminum, to manufacture and market its European-made aluminum tubes for the auto industry. Apart from its petroleum division, Norsk Hydro now has substantial interests in grain, foodstuffs, aluminum, magnesium and industrial chemicals.

Nationalized Companies

A study by the Federation, a Norwegian business group, concluded that there was a "substantial advance" in state ownership in industry in Norway during the 1970s. The state share of industry almost doubled in eight years, rising from 18 percent to 30 percent from 1970 to 1978—without even including the oil sector. Now state-owned companies occupy "the key positions in the nation's economy," the report concluded—a dramatic socialist achievement generally unrecognized in the United States.

AUSTRIA

Austria is the Western European nation with perhaps the largest state-owned sector. Austrian nationalization goes back to 1946, when plants, banks, and offices seized from the Nazis were nationalized. Into the state sector were swept the two largest banks, along with most of the nation's oil, chemicals, mining, heavy engineering, and steel industries.

The 1970s were an era of restructuring. In 1970, the government set up a holding company for the scores of diverse nationalized firms. OIAG (Osterreichische Industrieverwaltungs AG) was modeled on the Italian IRI, and all its shares are still held by the state. OIAG set out to combine and concentrate sectors—the four steel-producing companies were merged into VÖEST-Alpine, along with two shipyards. Producers of nonferrous metals were merged into one firm.

Concentration in the 1970s has been accompanied by diversification. Chemie Linz, the chemical arm of OIAG, has moved increasingly out of fertilizers into synthetics and basic chemicals. State firms were originally restricted to producing basic products and forbidden from expanding into higher value-added fields, especially consumer goods. But this restriction has now been largely removed, over the vocal objections of private manufacturers who complain about unfair competition from firms that are vastly subsidized, yet continue to record losses. VÖEST-Alpine, the largest Austrian firm and the largest exporter, has been operating at a loss for years. State firms are entering new sectors, including joint ventures with German firms for developing integrated circuits and microelectronics. The state banks have been called on occasionally to rescue failing firms.

The state now owns five of the nine largest Austrian firms. In the sixth, it has a large minority position. And of the remaining three, two belong to Austria's largest bank, in which the state owns a majority of the stock.

SWEDEN

Sweden has long served as the prototype for the modern welfare state. Its progressive income taxes, strong unions, Keynesian fiscal policy, and comprehensive social services testified to Sweden's commitment to social welfare. In the 1950s and 1960s, the Swedes saw little need for state ownership of industry. Liberals pointed with pride to what Sweden had accomplished without sacrificing the pluralism of a mixed economy. But by 1980, Sweden's reputation as the world's most efficient welfare state began to tarnish. One company after another in key industries faced bankruptcy. The Swedish state came to the rescue.

Until the 1970s, Sweden's attitude toward state-owned industry had been fairly hard-nosed. Sweden established a state holding company, whose purpose was to separate state-owned firms—then a motley collection of mostly small enterprises—from political interference. Sweden wanted to show that its state-owned firms could be enterprising, judged by the traditional economic test of profitability. The intent was to free managers from the constant interference of politicians, especially on matters of pricing, employment, and investment so that the firms could operate efficiently. The establishment of Statsforetag was followed by the government assumption of ownership of all pharmacies and purchase of Pripps, Sweden's largest brewery, in 1974. Statsforetag now has about thirty enterprises with 200 subsidiaries.

Sweden's real economic problems began in 1975 with the worldwide depression in the shipping industry. Sweden's shipbuilding industry, among the world's largest, fled into the state's hands, piece by piece, culminating in the establishment of state-owned Svenska Varv in 1977 and the takeover of the last shipyard to remain in private hands, Kockums, in 1978. The steel industry, traditionally one of Sweden's most competitive, came under state control in 1977, with the establishment of Swedish Steel, 50 percent state-owned, into which the loss-making steel companies were merged. The government also took over the two large clothing and textile concerns in 1977 and 1978. In addition, the two largest pulp and paper manufacturers needed government assistance, with the result that the state took a 73 percent interest in the firm NCB and 40 percent in Sodra. Meanwhile, the state set up a mini-computer company, Svenska Data, jointly owned with Saab-Scania (returned to private ownership in 1981).

Ironically, these expansions of state ownership in the economy occurred with the nonsocialist parties in power, parties elected on their promise to roll back Swedish socialism. The Swedish conservatives, faced with widespread economic crises of industry, nationalized more property in four years than the Social Democrats had in forty-four years.

The factor precipitating most of the Swedish nationalization in the 1970s was the difficulty faced by major Swedish export oriented industries. Sweden's high-priced labor and social benefits made most of Sweden's industry uncompetitive, raising serious questions about how Swedish industry could retain its position in world markets. Remaining competitive requires large infusions of capital for modernization which under present conditions are not forthcoming from the private sector. Hence, capital formation will become the major political issue in Sweden for the 1980s. Should the Swedish government itself provide the capital, via major new stakes in industry? How will the proposed "collective capitalism" of broader worker shares in industry, controlled by the unions, be attempted? These questions now divide Swedish socialists and nonsocialists more sharply than any other issue.

CURRENT SCOPE OF STATE OWNERSHIP

The mix of private and state ownership of industry varies somewhat from country to country in Western Europe. The estimate of the size of the state sector in an economy can vary widely, depending on the measurement one chooses: (1) percentage of physical capital (investment) owned by state enterprises; (2) percentage of total output; or (3) share of the labor force working in state companies. We have learned to exercise a healthy skepticism toward government statistical reports. Many government-owned companies are classified for statistical purposes as part of the private sector, and employees of some state-owned companies often are not counted as part of public sector employment. The result is that official reports on the size of the state-owned sector tend, sometimes dramatically, to understate its size. Our estimates of aggregate state ownership investment are given in Table 1. The data of these estimates—imperfect as they are—are collected from government statistical official reports and supplemented by other sources.

Table 1
PUBLIC SECTOR INVESTMENT AS
PERCENTAGE OF NATIONAL TOTAL

Austria	65
France	55
Italy	45
Norway	40
Sweden	30
Great Britain	25
Germany	20

Better data are available on the extent of state ownership at the industry level, despite the usual problems of defining the parameters of an industry and measuring the state firm's market share (by percentage of production, added value, employees, or investment). The recent trend toward diversification of state-owned firms into many different lines of business and the absence of line-of-business accounts make it impossible to measure the state's market share.

With these methodological reservations in mind, we can proceed to review the findings of various studies. One useful overview of state ownership of ten basic industries in ten Western European countries appeared in *The Economist*, December 30, 1978. As reproduced in Table 2, it demonstrates the overwhelming dominance of state ownership in the public utilities and transportation sectors— postal service, telephone service, electricity, gas, railways, and airlines. The more traditional industrial sectors of steel, motor vehicles, and shipbuilding show a considerable state stake as well. Developments since this table was compiled have increased the state's industrial stake substantially.

Nationalized Companies

Table 2
Scope of state ownership

Exhibit I
Scope of state ownership

	Posts	Tele-communications	Electricity	Gas	Oil production	Coal	Railways	Airlines	Motor industry	Steel	Ship-building
Australia											NA
Austria											NA
Belgium					NA						
Brazil											
Britain											
Canada											
France					NA						
West Germany											
Holland					NA	NA					

The Spreading Nationalization of European Industry

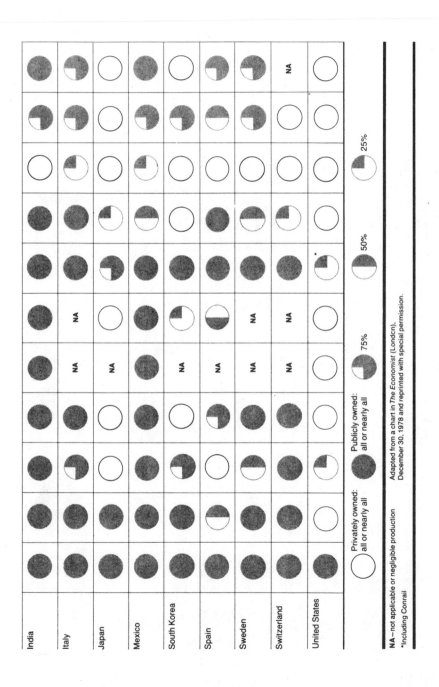

Table 3
SOME MAJOR STATE-OWNED INDUSTRIAL COMPANIES IN WESTERN EUROPE

Aerospace	Aluminum	Automobiles	Biotechnology	Chemicals	Computers and Electronics	Engineering	Mining (Coal and Metals)	Paper and Wood Products	Petroleum	Pharmaceuticals	Steel
Aérospatiale (France)	Ardal og Sunndal Verk (Norway)	Alfa Romeo (Italy)	British Petroleum (Britain)	ANIC (Italy)	C11-Honeywell Bull (France)	DIAG (Germany)	Charbonnages de France (France)	Assi (Sweden)	British National Oil Corporation (Britain)	Merieux (France)	British Steel (Britain)
Airbus (France)	EFIM (Italy)	BL Ltd. (Britain)	Celltech (Britain)	Berol Kemi (Sweden)	Eurotechnique (Australia)	Elin (Italy)	Enterprise Minière et Chimique (France)	Chapelle-Darblay (France)	British Petroleum (Britain)	Parcor (France)	Cockerill (Belgium)
Alitalia (Italy)	Gränges Aluminum (Norway)	BMW (Germany)	Elf-Aquitaine (France)	Beroxo (Sweden)	Inmos Limited (Britain)	Italimpianti (Italy)	IRI (Italy)	Enso-Gutzeit (Finland)	CFP-Total (France)	Sanofi (France)	Finsider (Italy)
British Aerospace (Britain)	Norsk Hydro (Norway)	Renault (France)	Rhône-Poulenc (France)	BP Chemicals (Britain)	International Computers Ltd. (Britain)	IVG (Germany)	LKAB (Sweden)	NCB (Sweden)	Danish Oil and Gas (Denmark)		Italsider (Italy)
CASA (Spain)	Pechiney (France)	SEAT (Spain)	Transgene (France)	CFP-Total (France)	Logabax (France)	Salzgitter (Germany)	ÖMV (Germany)	Södra Skogsägarna (Sweden)	Elf-Aquitaine (France)		Norsk Jernverk (Norway)
Dassault (France)	Ranshofen-Berndorf (Austria)	Volkswagen (Germany)		Charbonnages de France-Chimie (France)	Luxor (Sweden)	SERI (France)	National Coal Board (Britain)		ENI (Italy)		NJA (Sweden)
Matra (France)	VIAG (Germany)	Volvo Car (Netherlands)		DSM (Netherlands)	Matra (France)	Snamprogetti (Italy)	Ruhrkohle (Germany)		Neste (Finland)		Saarbergwerke (Germany)
Rolls-Royce (Britain)	Vereinigte Metallwerke (Austria)			Elf-Aquitaine (France)	Perter (Germany)	Technip (France)	Saarbergwerke (Germany)		ÖMV (Austria)		Sacilor (France)
SNECMA (France)				ENI (Italy)	SGS-Ates (Italy)	Valmet (Finland)			Saarbergwerke (Germany)		Salzgitter (Germany)
				Entreprise Minière et Chimique (France)	St. Gobain (France)	VÖEST-Alpine (Austria)			Statoil (Norway)		Swedish Steel (Sweden)
				Neste (Finland)	STET (Italy)				Swedish Petroleum (Sweden)		Usinor (France)
				Norsk Hydro (Norway)	Systime (Britain)				VEBA (Germany)		VEW (Austria)
				ÖMV (Austria)	Telub (Sweden)						VÖEST-Alpine (Austria)
				Saarbergwerke (Germany)	Thomson-Brandt (France)						
				VEBA (Germany)	VÖEST-Alpine (France)						

In Table 3, we have constructed a list of major state firms in various industries, including several industries not mentioned in Table 1—aerospace, aluminum, chemicals, computers and electronics, paper and wood products, and petroleum. Each year new firms have been added to this table as new companies were nationalized and existing state firms entered new markets. A report published in the *Financial Times* reveals the extent to which the 1982 French nationalizations dramatically increased the state share of manufacturing industry in France (Table 4).

Table 4
FRENCH STATE SHARE OF MANUFACTURING*
BY SALES

	Before	After
	Nationalization	
	%	%
Steel	1	80
Metalworking	13	63
Base chemicals	23	54
Synthetic textiles	0	75
Plastics	4	15
Fine chemicals	5	14
Pharmaceuticals	9	28
Glass	0	35
Construction materials	1	8
Cardboard	0	9
Foundry	4	22
Machine tools	6	12
Capital goods	3	14
Heavy engineering	0	5
Arms	58	75
Computer and office equipment	0	36
Power generating equipment	0	26
Electronics	1	44
Consumer durables	0	25
Shipbuilding	0	17
Aircraft	50	84
All manufacturing	18	32

*Does not include petroleum, banking, transportation, public utilities, and insurance.

Nationalized Companies

The data summarized in Tables 1–4 point to several conclusions. First, we estimate that state ownership in Western Europe is becoming the rule, not the exception, in a number of industries including aerospace, chemicals, and petroleum. A further conclusion is that state ownership continues to expand beyond the public utilities and transportation sectors, typically nationalized three decades or more ago, into the industrial and manufacturing sectors. In Western Europe at this time, the state has an ownership stake in twenty-nine of the fifty largest industrial companies. Investment in government-owned enterprises accounts for nearly one-half or more of all investment in several nations—among them, Austria, Norway, France, and Italy.

WHY EUROPE NATIONALIZES

The stream of new nationalization in Europe in the 1970s is perplexing since so much evidence suggests that nationalized companies perform less efficiently than their privately owned counterparts. How can this continuing wave of nationalization be explained? Are the answers to this question in economics, politics, history, or some complex combination of the three?

From an American political perspective, two factors stand out. First is the sheer number and ingenuity of arguments made for bringing an ever-larger proportion of industry under state ownership. Second, the arguments for and against nationalization heard in Europe tend to be accompanied by a remarkably high level of emotion and zeal. To penetrate beyond the almost evangelical tone of campaign promises in order to understand the underlying causes of recent nationalization is a formidable, but important, challenge.

ECONOMIC NATIONALISM

To most Americans, the notion that cabinet members and top government bureaucrats would study individual industries to choose the economic sectors and companies that showed special promise for economic growth seems inappropriate. Nearly everyone in the U.S. has traditionally felt that this is a task for companies themselves, not for governments. Organizations such as Japan's Ministry for International Trade and Industry (MITI) and Britain's National Economic Development Office (NEDO), which map out national and international strategies for various sectors of the national economy, are "foreign." When the international competitiveness of American industry is declining, as is now the case, the political dialogue calls primarily for tax changes, changes in labor policy and contracts and less regulation of business. The United States is less inclined to talk about, much less adopt, far-ranging industry-specific reforms—at least not compared with its trading partners in the Western industrialized world. However, the outcome of the present "industrial policy" may presage a fundamental shift in American ideology and policy.

But the U.S. position is not given much credence in Europe. Europeans tend to believe that it is possible to choose a number of sectors where a nation has a particular advantage in international trade and use appropriate government financial backing and public policy measures to help those sectors achieve international leadership. They argue that governments should do everything they can to build on a nation's inherent strengths, not only at the general level of encouraging all businesses, but also at the specific industry level.

A national industrial strategy does not have to include nationalization. Preferential government purchasing, loans and loan guarantees, straight financial assistance, export credits, tariffs and quotas, tax credits, and a variety of preferences to specific industries, are all part of a government's toolkit. Indeed, the recent expansion of state ownership of business has proceeded in tandem with many of these other forms of subsidy. State subsidies to industry and protections (the so-called nontariff barriers to trade) have proliferated. At a time when "visible protectionism" in the form of outright tariffs and quotas has been reduced, governments are finding new ways of protecting and promoting national industries. The proliferation of state-owned companies is but one manifestation of the trend toward economic nationalism, albeit a highly significant one.

In many ways, the state firm is the perfect instrument of economic nationalism—an organization that can be totally controlled by the government and is capable of behaving in a completely nationalistic fashion. One of the most-discussed political objections to private companies, particularly multinationals, is that they can easily behave in ways contrary to the national interest: They invest abroad at will, they purchase from lowest-cost suppliers without regard to nationality, and they seek generally to minimize costs (by seeking cheap labor abroad for example). Comparatively little thought is explicitly given to the national employment and welfare. *A la* Adam Smith, the private firm believes it is best serving the national interest when it follows its own rules of operating efficiently and profitably. A state-owned firm, on the other hand, can be told to keep investment at home, purchase from domestic suppliers, hire a nation's workers, and behave in an overtly nationalistic fashion so as to make the government look good. Greece's Andreas Papandreou's disdain for the self-serving policies of the multinational capitalist firms matches that of Anthony Wedgwood Benn in Britain and François Mitterrand in France. Nationalism and nationalization (or "socialization") appear increasingly as identical twins in political rhetoric.

The result is an enlarged role for nationalized companies in "national economic policy" to achieve specific national goals. Governments today cannot escape responsibility for directing the course of a nation's industry. No nation accepts relative economic decline with equanimity. A government cannot appear to be letting its major companies and industries decline and its markets be taken over by foreign producers without doing something. In political terms, it is simply not sufficient to tell companies to "stand on your own feet and compete." This is especially true since there is a widespread perception that countries that have broken the rules of international trade and imposed surreptitious subsidies and restrictions have done very well indeed. France allows the Japanese 3 percent of its car market, with more promised if and when Japan buys more French cars. Japan is delighted to import raw materials and luxury goods, but in markets where it is a major producer it has invented ingenious means to keep imports to levels it sees as being in its interests.

INTERNATIONAL COMPETITION

Closely allied with economic nationalism is the concept that nationalization is the best way for a nation to compete successfully in international markets. Although this matter is discussed in detail in Chapter 7, it must be noted briefly here as one of the major reasons for recent nationalization. As governments have faced increasing constraints on methods of achieving their industrial ends, they have opted to use state firms to carry out their industrial policies. When tariffs are reduced and quotas are outlawed (in name, if not always in practice) and other industrial policies are declared illegal, governments have sought invisible ways of subsidizing domestic industry to keep out imports and promote exports. Taxes and subsidies are less visible with state firms, and many government-firm relationships never become matters of public record at all. The ability to monopolize home markets yields gains in terms of trade—as long as other nations do not retaliate or insist that the trade treaties be strictly enforced.

Europe, like the United States, became much more vulnerable to international competition in the 1970s, and to shifts in the prices of raw materials, especially oil. Thus, it wanted an industrial policy that could develop national sources of supply for major industries. Nationalization has increasingly become the centerpiece of industrial policy in Europe. A whole series of industrial strategies for individual sectors of industry, some with greater priority than others, has emerged. These strategies are worked out with officials of government, industry, and sometimes unions. The aim is to improve the international competitiveness of the industry.

The Japanese and French appear to be the most successful practitioners of the art of industrial policy, perhaps because of their similarly elitist structures in government and business. All of the French political parties, with the single exception of the Communist party, are dominated by graduates of the grandes écoles—the Socialists, the Gaullists, and the center-right parties which supported Valery Giscard d'Estaing in the 1981 French election. Only a few people are required to make the decisions; they are in touch with each other regularly; and they act with a consciousness of collective responsibility for the national effort in international competition.[1] Thus, industrial and economic programs are developed and carried out with speed and remarkably little obstruction. When the Japanese decide that an economic sector is incapable of being internationally competitive, the government expeditiously cuts it back. Working in cooperation with the banks, Japan rechannels investment into what are deemed to be industries of the future. If the French decide that steel and textiles must be cut back, and telecommunications, aerospace, electronics, and biotechnology expanded, this is done, quickly and without protracted debate. In fact, it is scarcely a partisan matter—Gaullist policies would have been called "socialist" if introduced by Socialists William Pfaff notes.[2]

The basic assumptions of the rules of free trade are violated in the process, but this is hardly a matter of concern to the offenders. Their strategy has not been discovered by many American policymakers, much less countered. And the EEC, ostensibly the guardian of the free market in Europe, did nothing to halt the triumphal march of French nationalization.

RESCUES AND EMPLOYMENT MAINTENANCE

One frequent reason for recent nationalizations is the political need to rescue failing firms, thereby saving jobs and production. The British government took over British Leyland, Rolls-Royce, British Shipbuilding, and many of the smaller ownership stakes of the National Enterprise Board, to avoid the political problems that accompany layoffs following plant shutdowns. The French government's takeovers of the steel and chemicals industries were rescues, as were Sweden's many takeovers in the late 1970s.

In Europe, when a company faces bankruptcy, the employees want the government to take it over. They are not willing to accept major industrial restructuring without a political blood-letting, and successive legislation throughout Europe has enhanced employees' rights and limited management's freedom to make changes in working arrangements. Formal and informal systems of worker participation reinforced these trends. Companies are less able to react speedily to changing market conditions, and often unions and employees have what amounts to the power of veto over many decisions. Reconciling the aspirations of European employees with the requirements of competitive and flexible industry is an impossible task. The path of least political resistance has often been nationalization.

The tough question of whether declining industries and companies should be cut back to more efficient levels of production, or perhaps allowed to go bankrupt, to the ultimate advantage of the stronger and more promising sectors of the economy, is rarely resolved by market forces. Resuscitations, or slow deaths, via nationalization appear to be more popular politically. The reluctance to fire workers, to shut down large factories, to allow a company to fall into foreign hands—these are powerful political factors which make nationalization extremely attractive in the short run. The longer-run problems created by nationalization can be overlooked. Nationalization has rarely restored the patients to health; rather, the firms become addicted to annual subsidies, favored low-interest rates for investment, protection from imports, and the assured government purchases. This scenario, endlessly repeated, means that nationalization has become a politically fashionable alternative to bankruptcies, even though it has often been an expensive way to purchase job security.

Nationalized Companies

INVESTMENT AND ECONOMIC GROWTH

Another major reason for recent European nationalization is Europe's decreasing attraction for new private capital. When the outlook for return on private investment is poor, the state steps in to fill the gap. The reasons Europe is losing its attraction for new investment capital are numerous: Wage increases have tended to exceed productivity; governments are unwilling to let large inefficient firms fail; labor is reluctant to accept automation; management tolerates featherbedding; unemployment benefits approach full wage levels; legislation and union contracts severely restrict the ability of companies to realign jobs. All told, a climate of rising costs and deteriorating profit margins are not an auspicious environment for attracting investment. Well before the victory of the socialist-communist government in France, investment in the private sector tapered off, as investors and companies lived in fear of a left-wing victory. Subsequent political events confirmed their worst fears.

Of equal importance is the threat of nationalization itself. Threats of nationalization have become a self-fulfilling prophecy. One argument for nationalization is that private firms are not investing sufficiently in new plant and equipment. Yet, the possibility of nationalization drastically increases the risk of a given investment. British, German, and French investors have poured money into Switzerland and the United States because of nervousness over political risks in their own homelands. In a curious ideological twist, even some pension funds of state-owned industries in Great Britain have become major investors in the U.S. commercial real estate market. Where allowed by their governments, businesses in Europe are stepping up the pace of investment outside their own countries, and U.S. businesses have reevaluated their European investment strategies.

In the past, the state-owned sector grew because private enterprise was unable, or unwilling, to invest in some areas—transportation and communications networks, power projects, natural resources exploration—which were vital to the economy. Public enterprise can thus be seen as part of the infrastructure that helps private enterprise develop and prosper. Belief in risk-sharing runs deep in the socialist psyche. Lacking a strong financial base, European nations increasingly rely on governments to mobilize capital for large projects. Foreign investors are discouraged from investing by cries that foreigners seek to dominate the industry.

In short, lack of private investment increases the role of the state sector. Governments continue to take new economic initiatives and operate new industries that would otherwise be privately owned and managed. The result is that state-owned enterprises not only are now a major provider of industrial infrastructure but are major venture capitalists as well.

SOVEREIGNTY

Prime Minister Thatcher proposed in 1981 to sell a minority interest in the British National Oil Corporation, the company set up to develop Britain's North Sea oil resources. This provoked the wrath of Labour party leader Michael Foot, who declared: "We shall fight with every power in our being to protect British interests, and we will restore to British control everything you give away." Anthony Wedgwood Benn, as deputy secretary of the Labour party, said that the proposal would mean that multinational oil companies, especially American ones, would divert supplies out of Britain. Only 100 percent state ownership would guarantee state control.

The desire to maintain domestic ownership of strategic industries is a powerful argument for nationalizing certain industries—although the word "strategic" here means simply important, not directly defense-related. The Canadian program of nationalization of a large share of energy resources is a prime example. Prime Minister Trudeau did not even bother to conceal his hostility to international ownership in his overt attacks on foreign investment in the Canadian oil and gas industry. Norway's purchase of Alcan Aluminum's assets and of British Petroleum's holdings reflected a desire to wrest control of industries from foreign hands. Strong nationalist rhetoric can be very effective politically. Few nations are left in the world where major oil companies can have a stake in the ownership of oil.

French President François Mitterrand repeatedly appeals to French nationalism by stating that the French government must own major French companies in order to save them from the multinational corporations. Since the election, he has stressed this argument and offered fewer ideological justifications for nationalization.

> I am opposed to an international division of labor and production, a division decided far from our shores and

obeying interests that are not our own. We are not a pawn in the hands of those who are more powerful than we. This must be made clear, and for us nationalization is a weapon to protect France's production apparatus.[3]

One of Mitterand's early ministers, Jean-Pierre Chévènement, flatly stated that his mission was to save France from international capitalism and the multinational corporations. If the trends set in motion by Valery Giscard d'Estaing continued, he proclaimed, French culture would become folklore. All that would be left would be a few courageous holdouts in the mountains, clinging to their camemberts, baguettes, and bottles of wine. The multinationals would make the French speak English and populate France with international hotels and airports. The France of Giscard d'Estaing, Chévènement said, was France "in 1940 . . . exhausted . . . about to hand itself over to the United States."[4] Quite aside from their political appeal such comments are hardly calculated to encourage the free flow of commerce and investment. They serve as warnings that nationalization can occur, often suddenly, because of politically inflamed resentment over foreign ownership of industry.

POLITICS AND IDEOLOGY

Nationalization has meaning far beyond the formal economic theory. Nationalization in democratic Western Europe is fundamentally a political issue, a decision made by politicians who take their cues from the voters, not the marketplace. Passionate arguments and promises are advanced in favor of nationalization, and the debate on both sides of the issue is characterized by a high degree of emotion. No reform is of equal importance to bring about "a complete break with capitalism," the victorious French Socialist party proclaimed in its party congress in Valence in October 1981. Wherever nationalization is mentioned in leftist circles, revolutionary phrases such as "class struggle" and "treason of the bankers" are put forward to stir the passions of the left.

But politics is more than rhetoric; for the victors, it is also policy, as the 1981 election in France attests. The political campaign of Mitterrand exposed the political and ideological arguments for much of the nationalization that has occurred in recent European history. A number of ideological appeals in favor of nationalization were raised in the Common Program of the French Socialist and Communist parties. First, nationalization was necessary "to break the domination of big capital" and to usher in a "new economic and social policy." This is the classical Marxist analysis still advanced by most of the left throughout Europe as to the locus of economic power and political influence in capitalist societies. The premise is that capitalists dominate and exploit the working class ("The Golden Rule of Marxism is that those who have the gold make the rules.") It follows that the capitalists must be dislodged from their strongholds by divesting them of their claim to the "commanding heights" (industrial and financial core) of the economy. The fact that executives in private industry are adamantly opposed to nationalization gives politicians on the left—even those who prefer private ownership of industry, like Michael Rocard—additional reasons to support nationalization. The voting public that has not seen any perceptible increase in its well-being can be persuaded that the largest "centers of capitalist accumulation" must be taken into state ownership in order that the profits that end up in the hands of the monied elite that run capitalist societies should "belong to all the people."

The profound symbolic meaning of nationalization for the left throughout Europe can hardly be overstated. It is the major issue separating Anthony Wedgwood Benn from the centrist and rightist factions in the British Labour party. For moderate socialists in France, nationalization became a litmus test of their allegiance to an authentically "leftist," rather than a mere "reform," ideology, and an unnegotiable precondition to any successful electoral alliance with the left of the French Socialist party and the Communists. For the left of the French Socialist party, nationalizations are nothing more nor less than the "carrying out of the promises made by the left to the working class in 1936." For the Communists, nationalization is synonymous with expropriation of the wealth of the capitalist class and a concrete embodiment of their rhetoric since the founding of European Communist parties in the 1920s.

But in addition to these ideological arguments, other, more objective promises, are advanced in behalf of nationalization. French Socialists portrayed nationalization as one way (for some, the only way) of ensuring worker participation in industry. Factions disa-

greed over the degree of participation desirable, calling for everything from simple consultation in day-to-day management to uto-
pian schemes of worker control of top management and of the entire
enterprise. Furthermore, nationalized companies are expected to
become models for the rest of the economy and showplaces for improved working conditions, wages, job security—and in creating
many new jobs as well. The hopes that Socialist and Communist
candidates pinned on nationalization have become somewhat disappointing. Indeed, it has been reported that some French workers
became crestfallen a few months following the Mitterrand victory
in France when working conditions and living standards had
not improved overnight. Mitterrand had proclaimed: "Believe in jus-
tice and in happiness—that is the message of the Left." But
workers were impatient as to when, if ever, these ideals would become
reality.

John Redwood begins his insightful book *Public Enterprise in Crisis* with the statement: "Nationalization is part of a process by which
Socialists hope to create greater equality amongst men."[5] The reason
for nationalization can only be understood by recognizing the profound antagonism that has existed between the upper and working
classes in Western Europe for centuries. (The United States has
been largely spared this vestige of feudalism, as feudal notions were
anathema to the Founding Fathers, and any imported ideology of
inherent class distinction was largely dispelled by the belief in up-
ward mobility and meritocracy.) The contempt of the left-wing British intellectuals for the wealth and lifestyles of the upper class is
clearly seen in such works as R. H. Tawney's *The Acquisitive Society*.[6] Tawney advocates nationalization of industry to stop the upper
class from pursuing its life of ease at the expense of the laboring
class. "Properly conceived, [the] object [of nationalization] is not to
establish state management of industry, but to remove the dead
hand of private ownership, when the private owner has ceased to
perform any positive function." Tawney's contribution to Fabian
socialism combined Christian spirituality with the stern work ethic
of Calvinism to attack the drones of the upper class. The workers
had less incentive to work when the fruits of their labors were squan-
dered by men and women of leisure, who lived lives of conspicuous
idle pleasure. This social structure was fertile ground for the seeds
of Marxism. It is one of history's ironies that a nation has traded
its Protestant ethic for the "British disease" of embarrassingly low

productivity. Despite Tawney's dream of creating a new society of diligent workers with no more drones, the drone syndrome has become surprisingly pervasive. Unfortunately for Fabian idealism, a more productive society has not been created, nor have class antagonisms abated as promised. Nonetheless, this ideology still attracts a devoted following advocating further nationalization.

WHO CONTROLS
THE NATIONALIZED
COMPANY?

Close observation of Western Europe's nationalized companies over a period of years reveals one very clear point: Nationalized firms are almost always the tools of the politicians. Perhaps one could expect this. Although political interference in state firms is often denied, or even prohibited by law, the political goals of politicians take precedence over the policies of professional management, whenever there is a conflict. Indeed, the common discomfort of almost all managers of nationalized firms is their lack of operating autonomy in the face of political control.

The issue is understandable. Politicians want to be elected, and voters hold them—not the firms' managers—ultimately responsible for the nationalized companies' economic and political performance. Governments in power are eager to take credit when state companies do well, and they must also reluctantly take the political blame when the firms perform poorly. Elected governments in power are the closest thing to specific "owners" that the state firms have.

WHAT IS "GOVERNMENT CONTROL"?

When we assert that governments *control* nationalized firms, precisely what do we mean? We are not suggesting that managers have no function at all, or that they make no decisions, or that they must constantly check with politicians on even minor decisions. The two critical questions are: (1) What *kinds* of decisions are the managers allowed to make, and (2) what criteria guide them in these decisions? The government control of nationalized companies that we found can be expressed in three general principles:

(1) *Governments control ends (goals), although managements may control to some extent the means to achieve those ends.* This concept of managerial autonomy is that emphasized by Pierre Dreyfus, as chairman of Renault.[1] Government sets the state company's goals and objectives, yet management is given considerable freedom as to how to implement the government's wishes. Freedom to carry out government policies is not complete, however. Dreyfus stresses the need for continuing dialogue and communication between the top government leaders and the chief executive officers of the nationalized companies. This implies that the government wants not only to monitor the firms but also to make its feelings known to the top management on an ongoing basis.

(2) *Management proposes, but government disposes.* This rule has been articulated by the chairmen of several state companies who we asked to describe their operating relationship with the government. They added that on all *important* decisions the management not only consults with the government but must obtain government approval. It also recognizes that management must acquire from the government the financial resources necessary to implement many major decisions. The principle reserves for management the right to *initiate* policy but not to *make* policy.

(3) *Government retains effective decision making power whenever its political welfare is clearly at stake.* This principle recognizes that managers may have autonomy on any number of issues, but only insofar as management's decisions are consistent with the government's political interests. If the manager exercises autonomy so as to lead to a conflict with the government's wishes, the government intervenes and overrules. Shrewd managers appreciate this fact and avoid making decisions, or adopting policies, which invite conflict with a government. Managers have only the autonomy that governments give them. The degree of autonomy they enjoy is itself a government decision which can be altered at any time.

One could analogize that the top manager of a state-owned firm is like a university professor who is told that he has academic freedom as long as he does not say or do anything that is politically controversial. How much freedom is this? Some professors do not wish to speak or write about political matters at all; hence, they are entirely free to say or do whatever they like. Others would be so constrained that the grant of academic freedom ceases to have any significance. Similarly, the top management of the state firm is free to do any number of things as long as it keeps in mind that its owner and boss is the government. It is important for the manager to perceive fully the government's expectations of the firm, and to avoid making decisions that would embarrass the government, conflict with it, or show the government, or the firm, in a negative political light. It is in this sense that governments control nationalized companies, and it is much more formidable than visible to many outside observers. There are few limits to the pragmatic interventions in the policies of state firms by government, all justified by reference to the public interest.

HOW GOVERNMENTS EXERCISE CONTROL

Precisely how do politicians control the state-owned companies? Effective control is achieved through three processes: (a) appointment of the chief executive officer and the board of directors, (b) overt intervention in decision making when necessary, and (c) financial control. We will briefly examine each.

APPOINTMENT OF TOP MANAGEMENT

The most important means of control of state companies is the power of appointment of boards and the chief executive officer. If the chairman of a company is loyal to the government in office and sensitive to its political wishes, there is likely to be little conflict. But if the chairman does not understand that he is hired to serve the government, and behaves as if his boss were a group of private shareholders, disagreement and confrontation are certain. Governments know this and choose chief executives who are favorably disposed toward their policies and can be counted on to align the nationalized companies with those policies.

Throughout the postwar period, the issue of control over state firms has been handled with remarkable uniformity in Western Europe. The elected government in power appoints the board of directors of the state firm, including the chairman. Governments typically have the power to reappoint, or not to reappoint, chairmen and (with some possible difficulty) can remove from office the chairman and members of the board. The chairman of a large, privately owned company may wonder if his firm's financial performance will meet the criteria of the company's board, or of the stockholders, but the chairman of the state enterprise must ultimately please only one or two persons to keep his job—the Prime Minister, or President, and possibly also either the Finance Minister or the Minister who is formally charged with appointing him.

When the chairmen of state firms talk and write about their jobs, they fully grasp the lines of authority drawn in the organization chart: They are linked directly to the government. This chain of accountability is also periodically reestablished in case a chairman is under the illusion that the leash given him is longer than the government intends it to be.

The safest course for a government is to choose someone personally known and trusted to head the state companies. French President Giscard d'Estaing "parachuted" Claude Pierre-Brossolette, his personal aide, into the top post at Crédit Lyonnais, one of the large nationalized banks. Observers of state companies have often wondered why chairmen of nationalized companies are typically named from outside the ranks of the company's management. The reason is simple: The government likes to select someone in whom it can place full confidence and expect substantial loyalty.

Business executives in the state companies bristle at the tendency of heads of state to select executives who know nothing about an industry but are chosen mostly for their political loyalty or their close personal connections to the government. When Alastair Morton resigned as a senior executive director of British National Oil Corporation because he disliked the new chairman that Margaret Thatcher had named, he erupted: "The Prime Minister should realize that you cannot put together the management of major industrial corporations in the way you choose party political leaders." Morton failed to realize that the most effective way a government controls a nationalized company is by appointing a chief executive who will look out for the interests of the government and carry out its policies.

Sometimes the appointed chairman will come directly from the government's ranks, as in the recent case of Lufthansa, the German state airline company. Late in 1981, Lufthansa admitted paying illegal commissions to a West Germany travel agent to boost sales. The government, which holds 75 percent of Lufthansa's shares, stepped in and arranged for the board to appoint Heinz Ruhnau, the state secretary in the Transport Ministry in Bonn, as the new chairman, effective July 1, 1982. The outgoing chairman, whose contract ran

Nationalized Companies

until 1984, would leave for "health reasons," the board said. Lufthansa employees complained about what they claimed was "the politicization of the company," to no avail. The government put in an administrator that it fully knew and trusted.

The widespread nationalizations of the current French socialist government have reinforced government control over boards of directors. Under the Nationalization Bill, all board appointments of the companies nationalized were automatically terminated. Several company chief executives anticipated being terminated and resigned. Ambroise Roux, chairman of Compagnie Générale d'Electricité, told his board he would resign as soon as the Nationalization Bill became law because of his "attachment to the ethic of capitalism and the free market economy." The head of Crédit Commercial de France, J.-M. Lévêque, explained that it would be inconceivable for the government to reappoint him after his company was nationalized since he had been a vocal opponent of the electoral program of the Socialist party:

> I am president of a private enterprise, elected by a corporate board which is itself elected by a large group of shareholders. It seems to me inconceivable that the president could stay in place once these shareholders are eliminated. I am fundamentally hostile to the state-run economy. My position would be in contradiction with my opinions if I were at the head of an enterprise belonging to the state.[2]

Other chairmen of the newly nationalized firms were careful not to criticize the government's policies in hopes of keeping their jobs.

When an election brings a new party into power, a new group of chairmen of state companies can usually be appointed. The socialist ascendancy in France meant not only that there was a housecleaning of government officials but that the top levels of nationalized industry could be virtually swept clean as well. The closer a chief executive officer's relationship with the outgoing government, the more certain was his demise from power in his company. Claude Pierre-Brossolette, chairman of Crédit Lyonnais, was among the first to go because of his close relationship with ex-President Giscard d'Estaing. Only two chairmen of companies nationalized in France in the wake of the 1981 election kept their jobs. That two chairmen were kept infuriated the communist-controlled union CGT, which criticized the government for not making a "complete break with capitalist management."

Although there are a few exceptions, the appointments of chief executive officers of state-owned companies generally reflect political leanings, and even specific party affiliation. Certainly this is true in the recent appointments in France. The government's socialist policies are expected to be faithfully enacted by the new chief executives, who even include several hard-line socialists. The new French socialist government has been credited, however, for appointing people not only with socialist credentials but with business expertise and experience as well, in the time-honored French technocratic mold.

Using the state firms for explicit political patronage has proven to be one of the continuing practices (many say curses) of Italian industry. Outsiders are appointed to top posts in state companies on purely political grounds, frequently with few or no professional or industrial credentials. The Italian Communist party has repeatedly demanded that candidates be selected for top jobs in state industries on professional merit rather than on purely political considerations. But are the communists complaining only because they are out of power, and their members have not been chosen? There is ample evidence for precisely this, since where the Communist party controls city politics in Italy, it has been known to use political patronage also. Middle to senior managers throughout the Italian state industries continue to complain about patronage, but to little avail. The top appointments still are made by the party in power. The ample Italian state-owned sector provides many careers for party functionaries.

Coalition governments have a difficult time choosing the heads of a nation's nationalized companies. The tendency is to share the jobs among members of the various coalition parties, yet the struggles and logrolling are intense and not easily resolved. After the appointments are made, the pattern of control is also much less clear, since there is no single party in power. In March 1982, the Italian government's Minister of State Shareholdings demanded the resignation of the top management of ENI, including its president, Alberto Grandi. When Grandi refused to resign after serving less than two years of his three-year term, Gianni De Michelis named a "special commissioner" to run ENI as a temporary head. Political

Nationalized Companies

opponents sensed an attempt by De Michelis and his Socialist party to take control of the state energy conglomerate. With the game of political patronage unabashedly blatant in Italy's state companies, the other parties sharing power were eager to name their own loyalists to high positions in the state industries after long periods of solid Christian Democratic rule.

OVERT INTERVENTION IN DECISION MAKING

Another indication that governments control state firms is seen in those situations where a government's wishes have come in overt conflict with those of the state firm's management. Most conflicts never become public—especially in countries such as France and Germany where a high premium is placed on management's ability to discuss potential conflicts with the government secretly and without political damage. But even in such nations, it has been impossible to keep all conflicts from public view. Ten short examples, drawn from a number of countries, reveal a general pattern of government dominance and management subordinance that occurs when genuine clashes of will are manifest:

1) Sir Monty Finniston, as chairman of British Steel, announced in 1975 that the firm would reduce its labor force by 20,000 over a period of months, due to a slump in steel demand. The Secretary for Industry, Anthony Wedgwood Benn, immediately announced: "I do not accept that a publicly owned industry can behave as if it is a private concern of the Board or Management." Even though Finniston withdrew his plan, he was replaced the following year.

2) In 1975, the top management of Air France asked the French government, as it is legally obliged to do, for authorization to buy a fleet of Boeing 737 airplanes to replace the fleet of aging Caravelles. The answer was an immediate "no." The Minister of Finance soon delivered a public speech, accusing "certain public managers" of acting as if their company belonged to them and of not seeking the public interest. After long and tortuous negotiations between Air France management and the government, the government let Air France lease thirteen 737's, but Air France promised to buy Airbuses as soon as they became available.

3) In recent years both ENI and IRI, the two Italian state conglomerates, have had continuing rebellions among top management who complained that they had essentially no voice in running the firms.

A number of top managers resigned, claiming political interference had made their jobs impossible.

4) Per Skold, as chairman of Sweden's state holding company, Statsforetag, said in 1980 that although the company was legally charged with operating profitably, after ten years of operations the government had not yet decided the criteria by which Swedish state companies should be managed.

5) Margaret Thatcher, British Prime Minister, refused to give the state-owned microelectronics firm, Inmos, the £25 million it needed to build its manufacturing plant until the management agreed to build it in Wales, an area of high unemployment. The management had urged that the plant be in Bristol, until it became clear that the decision on plant siting was not its to make, but the government's.

6) In 1980, Egidio Egidi resigned as president of ENI a few days before he was formally scheduled to take office, because he opposed a plan for ENI to divest itself of a number of chemical companies, a proposal the Italian government backed.

7) The chairman of the Post Office in Great Britain, Sir William Barlow, resigned in 1980 because the government imposed tight financial limits on the company's borrowing, which restricted the Post Office's ability to expand into new technologies.

8) Albin Chalandon, the chairman of Elf-Aquitaine, the French state-owned oil company, wanted the company to diversify, particularly in the United States. When he took steps to acquire Kerr-McGee, a U.S. energy firm, the French government vetoed the idea. (Elf subsequently purchased Texasgulf, a policy the new socialist government favored.)

9) The New Zealand government rejected the request of the management of the Air New Zealand to buy General Electric engines for a new fleet of aircraft. The New Zealand Prime Minister explained that the government had decided in favor of Rolls-Royce engines and denied that other trade issues between Great Britain and New Zealand had dictated the outcome.

10) In the mid-1970s, Great Britain's Labour government adopted an incomes policy which asked industry to limit pay increases to £6 a week. Industry secretary Eric Varley stated in the House of Commons that if any nationalized industry gave an increase of more than £6 a week, its chairman would be dismissed. (A related incident occurred two years later when British state firms were instructed

Nationalized Companies

to refuse to purchase from private-sector companies that violated the government's pay guidelines.)

This list of ten cases of overt conflict is the tip of the iceberg, but it is typical of the general pattern of government control. Control looks formidable when one examines situations where government's wishes have conflicted with those of management. The important point is not whether government or management was "correct," but that government indeed overrules management whenever important conflicts occur. The best that management can do is try to change the government's attitude through quiet negotiation. For management to "go public" is to embarrass the government and guarantee that government will overrule it. If the disagreement between management and the government cannot be resolved, the outcome is simple and predictable: The government decides what the firm's policy will be. We have found virtually no exceptions to this rule.

The government's legal justification for intervention is that nationalized companies are being held accountable to their "owners," the citizen-voters. This argument, though legally correct, reveals the politicians' rejection of the traditional business concept of accountability. To a business executive, accountability means that a firm is evaluated according to financial standards. If the firm is to meet the competition of the market, managers must have freedom and flexibility to adopt policies that will achieve necessary returns. Hence, accountability and autonomy are not contradictory; managerial autonomy is necessary to achieve financial accountability and efficiency.

But to a politician, accountability is measured in political terms. Politicians are accountable to voters, and this accountability extends to all matters coming within the purview of the government, including the nationalized firms. The political scientist Anthony King argues that when politicians are held responsible for something, they intervene in it.[3] This creates chaos for the managers of the nationalized firms. Indeed, the most frustrating thing about managing a state company is that the latest political crisis or exigency dictates what the firms are expected to do. Politics has a short-term orientation that conflicts with the medium- and long-term planning needs of business enterprises. This planning is impossible when politicians can be counted on to interfere with the state firms' management, whenever they can gain political advantages by doing so.

It is possible that governments may have the best of intentions when they appoint new managers of the nationalized firms and assure them that they will have the right to manage. A newly appointed chairman of a state company characteristically announces that the government has conferred on him greater autonomy in decision making than his predecessor enjoyed. But these good intentions, like New Year's resolutions, soon collide with realities. The present socialist government in France has insisted all along that it planned to run the nationalized sector on a fairly loose rein. The managers were to have autonomy, and power would become more decentralized than under private ownership. President François Mitterrand publicly assured the new chairmen of the state companies that the government would not meddle in their affairs. The promise of decentralization was patently at odds with the electoral promises of the Socialist party to reassert control over the largest firms in the economy by nationalizing them. While Mitterrand talked of the need to wrest power from the hands of the capitalists and turn the power over industry back to the people and the workers, the fact remains that nationalization of large new sectors of an economy is fundamentally inconsistent with the decentralization of economic power.

FINANCIAL CONTROL

Government appointments and the specific directives and interventions in decision making are important means of controlling state-owned firms. An additional (many would say the most important) source of control stems from the financial dependency of the firms on the government. The power of the purse is a source of *de facto* power, unregulated by law. The persistence and size of the deficits of many state companies and their need for continual support from the government financial authorities give the government enormous power over the enterprises. Although a state-owned company may be legally responsible to the Minister of Industry, the company's CEO is likely to have more frequent contacts with and dependence upon the Minister of Finance. Numerous executives throughout Europe told us that for this reason their state companies in reality come under the authority of the Minister of Finance.

Government ownership of the banks, now virtually complete in France and well-advanced in Italy, gives it potential control over even the private sector of industry, at least insofar as private firms need loans for expansion and operations. The power to allocate credit in such a total and complete fashion is potentially awesome, and the way in which this power is used in France will be of considerable interest to observers of nationalization in the future.

WHAT DO GOVERNMENTS CONTROL?

What kinds of decisions do governments try to influence, and what areas of greater freedom are left to the firm? It is difficult to generalize accurately about these questions. Yet two general statements can be made. First, there are no areas of the firms' decision making that have not been subjected to political control at times. Second, whether particular controls and interventions in specific firms take place depends on political factors (i.e., when will the government benefit politically by controlling or intervening). Our discussion here will center on several specific areas of decision making in which governments have been especially prone to intervene.

PRICES

There is a no more tangled political issue than how much autonomy a government should give a state-owned firm to set its prices. Inflation is a serious problem in all economies, and politicians are anxious to stabilize prices by whatever means are available. The government can control prices of state firms it owns more directly and easily than it can control the prices of privately owned firms, so the state firms are handy targets for price controls. Calls for the private economy to exercise price and wage restraint look hypocritical if the government's own companies are leading the way in price increases. Furthermore, since the state companies often provide goods and services which are an important part of the cost-of-living index, price increases in state companies can have a multiplier-effect on the price level of the entire economy where labor contracts are tied to the cost-of-living index. Hence, the government is quite anxious to keep the prices of many of the state firms from rising too rapidly. It is especially anxious to do this in a preelection period, and, in fact, there is considerable historical evidence that state companies tend to nearly freeze their prices in the year before national elections and then raise them rapidly in the following year.

But governments know that keeping the lid on prices of state firms is not a "free lunch"—especially in the long run. If the companies' costs continue to rise faster than revenues, larger and larger deficits have to be financed by the government's budget, or by borrowing. The fundamental political problem to be faced by each government is: Should the state companies keep their prices down for political reasons, or should managers of the state firms be allowed to set prices to cover costs or to achieve a profit? Managers clamor for pricing freedom. But pricing freedom has often led to runaway prices—especially where the firms are outright state monopolies or are protected in other ways from competition. Britain's Prime Minister Thatcher believes that managers of state firms should have pricing freedom, as did Prime Minister Raymond Barre of France. Yet both have been at a loss to know how to keep the nationalized companies from passing on huge added costs to consumers through higher prices. Since the firms often have great market power, there is less incentive to keep costs under control.

Prices of the state-owned companies are almost always political issues. Giving the managers freedom to set prices does not absolve the government from political blame for price increases.

LABOR RELATIONS

Issues of labor relations in nationalized companies—wage levels, staffing requirements, and deployment of workers—create more political problems than political opportunities for governments. Governments often try to rid themselves of responsibility for the companies' labor difficulties and explicitly delegate such matters to the top managers of the company, but this seldom works. The unions usually figure out that they are ultimately bargaining with the company owner, the government—not the managers. Despite the government's efforts to keep aloof from labor squabbles, it will reluctantly, but usually, step in to resolve them when the issues become intractable and threaten other sectors of the economy. Government alone has the "deep pocket" (budget) to meet the claims of the workers.

That industrial relations should be so politicized in nationalized companies is surprising to those who first advocated nationalization as a means of vanquishing labor-management conflict. When the surplus-value extracted by capitalists was outlawed, it was thought, laborers would happily work for the public good. But after years of experience with state companies, labor problems in government-owned companies are more troublesome than in private companies. William A. Robson of the London School of Economics, an indefatigable long-term observer of the nationalized companies, states: "There has been ample demonstration that industrial relations deteriorate rather than improve when capitalism is replaced by public ownership, and that the unions are more ruthless when they negotiate with a public corporation rather than a private employer." He regretfully adds that "the most disturbing feature" of the state companies is "the complete absence of any sense of public spirit" among the workers.[4]

What accounts for the severe labor problems of nationalized companies? The main reason appears to be that politicians want both industrial peace and the workers' votes and so yield comparatively easily to the wage demands of state workers. Governments do not like strikes in the state companies—strikes inconvenience the public, disrupt commerce, and often draw them directly into bargaining with workers. The chairmen of the companies know that governments want to avoid the political hazards of strikes, so they have every incentive to calm the political waters by paying off the workers, so long as the price is not *too* high. Although there are some exceptions, time and again we have seen decision making power in industrial relations effectively transferred from the company management to the government. In perhaps the most dramatic case, the British national election in 1974 was fought principally over the issue of whether the coal miners should be given wage increases of 35 percent and the election cost Edward Heath the prime ministership.

Is it politically wise for governments to give in to public workers or to take a tougher line? It probably depends on the circumstances of the particular case. Thatcher's policy was to encourage British Steel's Ian MacGregor and BL's Sir Michael Edwards to take a far more aggressive line with employees than was customary in the past. This hard-nosed stance has paid off in the sense that the workers have retreated from their exorbitant wage claims and settled for substantially less in recent years. Yet Thatcher fled from a major challenge from the coal miners in 1981 and gave them what they wanted without a fight. In all these cases, the issues for Prime Minister Thatcher involved not only economic but political calculation as well.

Special insight on industrial relations in nationalized firms is shown by Dudley Jackson of Cambridge University, who blames excessive wage increases for the financial problems and lack of profitability of the nationalized companies. "The central issue in the control of public enterprises is . . . the determination of wages and salaries," he declares. He explains why wages tend to be comparatively high in state companies:

> In the private sector, collective bargaining is "realistic" in the sense that there tends to be a fairly clear-cut conflict of interest between profits and employee remuneration, and those on the owner/managerial side of the bargaining table have an interest in seeing that increases in employee remuneration are not "excessive." In public enterprise, on the other hand, the managerial side of the bargaining team will often be simultaneously determining, or indirectly influencing, increases to their own salaries, so that collective "bargaining" becomes something of a sham. Inevitably these problems of remuneration in public enterprise, and of the relation of pay in the corporations to pay in the civil service, preclude "independence" for the corporations. This important fact shapes much of . . . policy toward public enterprise.[5]

PURCHASING

A government-owned company is open to constant interference in purchasing decisions. For example, British Airways, the government-owned airline, recently purchased six wide-bodied jets. The three American companies competing for the sale, Boeing, Lockheed, and McDonnell Douglas, learned that politics played the biggest role in purchasing decisions for British Airways. "We had been fighting on a straight sales pitch to British Airways (the usual tactic in commercial aircraft sales), but we realized this wasn't enough," a McDonnell Douglas spokesman explained. The company redirected its sales effort at the ruling Labour party and the union officials who are especially influential with the Labour government. Despite its efforts, Lockheed won the contract with its well-placed gifts, to its eventual discomfiture and that of Prince Bernhard of the Netherlands and Prime Minister Tanaka of Japan. But government interference sets the stage for this kind of activity.

INVESTMENT

Private industry must convince stockholders and lenders that it can make a satisfactory return on the capital entrusted to it, but the nationalized firms' investment decisions reflect the preferences and pressures of government. In actual practice, investment decisions are usually made without being subjected to criteria of financial return. Improved service and increased productivity can result from large commitments of government funds to new investment, of course, but the intent is generally to seek technical efficiency and employment without any real expectation of profitability or explicit financial return to the state. Rescuing ailing enterprises is an area in which political pressures are keenly felt. High-level investment plans of all state companies have to be approved by the government. Explicit laws in Italy require state-owned companies to locate 60 percent of their existing investments and 80 percent of new investments in the Mezzogiorno, the area of southern Italy.

The impact of state-controlled investment policy is not fully known, but Franco Grassini argues that in Italy the managers of state-owned enterprises "are able to take higher risks in their investments than managers of private enterprises."[6] The economic performance of a state company does not reflect substantially on its management's performance, he explains, since "the only indicator of successful management is an increase in employment." Increases in employment can be guaranteed by government funds for new investment.

OTHER AREAS OF INTERFERENCE

In all other areas of decision making, governments have routinely intervened either overtly or covertly. Company policies on plant location and shutdown, diversification, incentive systems and executive compensation, product development, and financial policy have come under government control to a remarkable degree.

WHY GOVERNMENTS CONTROL THE STATE FIRMS

Given the ample evidence that governments control the policies of the state firms, an important question remains: Why? The one-word answer is: politics. Governments control the nationalized companies because it is in their political interest to do so.

It is a truism that politicians use whatever resources they have at their disposal to win votes. Modern governments spend an impressive share of the gross national product, and the opportunities for influencing the economy and the elections through fiscal and monetary policy are well documented. When a government also owns large companies, the opportunities for political manipulation are that much larger. The state firms can stimulate the economy prior to elections in order to enhance a government's prospects of being returned to office. Governments can use the nationalized firms to win votes.

The state firms' service of the short-term interests of politicians is often at the expense of the long-term interests of society. Even expertly advised governments cannot achieve all their objectives, and this is certainly true in controlling the state companies for political ends. What is important for politicians is for voters to perceive them as trying to do something about problems. Where the nationalized firms are conspicuously instructed by politicians to save jobs, invest in new technology, hold the line on domestic prices, export, and purchase domestic products over imports, the political benefits can be substantial. These are all "socially responsible" activities, which governments can contrast to the conduct of private firms. Voters have been told that while private firms are run for the personal greed of their owners, the state firms are following social criteria to maximize not profits but the public interest.

Governmental control of the state firms occurs as a result of two different kinds of circumstances. In one, state companies present a government with a political opportunity. In the second, state companies present a difficult political problem which requires the government to intervene. In the former case, the government rushes to intervene and takes credit for the firm's adoption of a politically popular policy. In the latter, the government may not be able foist the responsibility for an unpopular decision on the shoulders of others, or onto "circumstances," and hence must itself reluctantly intervene. In either case, voters hold the government "responsible"— it receives the credit or the blame.

What opportunities do the state firms present for government? A few of these most commonly cited by governments themselves can be listed briefly. Ministers sometimes hold up nationalized companies as a model of what industrial relations should be (e.g., Renault in France). Exports are high on the list of benefits that nationalized firms provide a nation's economy—a few very large companies, many of them nationalized, are in fact responsible for a high proportion of French and British manufactured exports. That nationalized companies must give preference to domestic suppliers is noted again and again by governments. Price restraint by the firms is also mentioned often—especially near election time.

Other political opportunities are more unexpected and curious, yet politicians are quick to seize them as well. El Al, the Israeli government-owned airline, serves only kosher food by government edict, and Prime Minister Begin promised a small party in his coalition that he would order El Al to cease flying on the Sabbath. These policies are explicitly at the government's decree, to the consternation of management. In another case, when British Rail decided to give up its costly policy of carrying stray racing pigeons, the chairman of British Rail received more than 250 protesting letters from MPs.

In addition to the cases where the state firms provide a politician with a "free political lunch," in other cases the state firms are more bane than blessing to the government in power. Governments often simply can't avoid dilemmas in which they find difficulty extracting any political benefits. As an article in the February 6, 1981 *Wall Street Journal* headlined, "Thatcher Government to Bail Out BL, Once More Defying Its Own Principles," pointed out:

> It isn't a new lesson being taught here—merely a new and striking demonstration of an old one: in a democracy, it is a lot easier for a government to start bailing out businesses than it is to stop. The economic, social, and political costs of stopping—the business failures and rising unemployment that result—may simply be too great to risk.

In addition to the embarrassment of continuing huge losses in the state firms, other kinds of bad news draw the government openly into the decision making process—strikes, layoffs, labor disputes, plant closures, and product line closures (as when BL dropped the Triumph). Governments get involved in these no-win decisions very reluctantly. They know that the bearer of bad news, no matter how accurate or necessary, is not beloved by voters—only by opposition politicians who will claim mismanagement. It is one thing to announce good news about nationalized companies—exports, new orders, employment, growth, and new technology; governments love to take credit for these developments. It is quite another to "manage" the negative performance of companies in a way that will minimize political damage. About all that can be done is to put the best face on matters, blame circumstances, and proclaim that better days lie ahead.

MANAGING THE NATIONALIZED COMPANY

How is managing a government-owned company different from managing a privately owned company? An initial insight into the managerial differences is summed up by one top executive's wry comment: "Running a nationalized company is like having a stockholders' meeting every day." He explained that government ministers, civil servants, or legislators were on the telephone almost daily, giving him opinions and instructions on how he should run the company. Indeed, the government ministers were tantamount to the owners—or stockholders—of the company. A chief executive officer's ultimate marching orders come, not from private investors who want to see the value of their stock increase, but from government officials who want to be reelected.

In one sense the top executive in a nationalized company is like a top executive in a firm wholly owned or controlled by one individual. The sole owner has the power to dictate policy to the manager anytime. In addition, the government minister, like a private owner, has the power to appoint the manager he or she chooses.

Yet the job of the chief executive officer of a nationalized company is not so much perilous as it is perplexing. The manager of the nationalized company is apt to have a somewhat different conception of how the company should be run than the politicians who control the government and who are evaluated by the public at election time. Politicians are intent on winning votes, and the state-owned firm can be either a vehicle or a threat to accomplish this purpose. By contrast, the managers we interviewed expressed their wish to run the company according to general business practices so that it can operate profitably, or at least not lose too much money.

Profit, however, is not likely to be the criterion by which the government judges the success of the nationalized firm. Politicians can insist that the manager fulfill numerous nonbusiness goals— keeping prices low, keeping employment up, rescuing failing firms, or any number of other goals that the politicians feel will appeal to the electorate. These goals divert the manager of the nationalized firm from the traditional economic preoccupations of the private firm. Prices may be set lower and costs may be allowed to rise higher for political reasons, rendering profit an unimportant goal for most nationalized firms. Managers are remarkably candid about the fact that they face conflicting goals and have to live with many opposing operational criteria as part of their jobs.

The managers generally complain that they have a harder job than the managers of private companies, but they are also aware that many of the financial pressures faced by private managers— such as making up deficits or gaining access to new loans—can be solved by the stroke of a pen in the hand of a government minister. The politically astute manager of the nationalized company can generally ride out economic storms that would cause the firing of almost any manager of a private corporation. Put more bluntly, privately owned firms have a low tolerance for continuing losses. Their survival depends on their being or becoming profitable. But if the manager of a nationalized company can keep the government happy with the company's *political* performance, he can stay on the job, even in the face of heavy losses. The manager's task is to determine what the company's best political performance might be.

A good example is state-owned British Airways in contrast to a privately owned airline such as Braniff. In the case of British Airways, recent huge losses resulted partially from overstaffing. British Airways ranks fifth in revenue on the basis of tons flown per kilometer (after United, American, Pan American, and TWA), yet it has by far the largest number of employees. While large losses in a privately owned firm caused Lawrence Harding at Braniff to be forced out of office and the company out of business, his counterpart, Roy Watts, deputy chairman and chief executive of British Airways, was not fired even under the conservative Thatcher government. Indeed, because Watts has convinced the Thatcher government that he can improve the efficiency of British Airways without disastrous political consequences, he has been given large government loans in an effort to attempt a major turnaround. As much as he may try to reduce an oversized work force, he is unlikely to bring British Airways to a point where it will be profitable. This illustrates a general pattern in the management of nationalized companies. Managers of state companies are not likely to be fired over large losses.

MANAGERS VS. MINISTERS: IS CONFLICT INEVITABLE?

A favorite proposal of political parties out of office is their promise to take the nationalized companies "out of politics" if they are elected. "The managers should run the nationalized companies," is a familiar political slogan. The implication is that the government in office is interfering too much in the affairs of the companies. This criticism is most likely to come from right-of-center parties out of power, but similar sentiments can be heard from left-of-center oppositions as well (candidate François Mitterand promised more autonomy for French state companies). But after parties promising greater management freedom take office, they tend to change their minds. Every major decision facing the management of the nationalized company potentially has the power to embarrass a government that voters perceive as handling (or failing to handle) it properly.

Some conflict between governments and managers of the state companies is inevitable. The successful manager will know how far to go in encouraging the government to see the company's point of view. He also must know when he should not even try to change the government's attitude, but obediently follow its wishes without complaint. Let us examine several major government interventions and see how managers have attempted to influence government policies on these issues.

PRICING

A repeated issue to be faced is whether managers should have pricing freedom. In the case of monopolistically supplied services, the case for pricing control is strong. But the nationalized companies operating in more competitive industries often find their freedom curtailed. Pierre Dreyfus at Renault complained that the price increases allowed by the authorities never kept pace with Renault's constant rise in costs. The high price of natural gas by the British Gas Corporation has been an unrelenting political headache of Margaret Thatcher's government, as the profits have been used to supplement the government's revenues, while business customers and private households scream. In an opposite case, Elf-Aquitaine's chairman Albin Chalandon has incessantly lobbied for pricing freedom for the French state-owned oil company, yet the government has insisted on controlling prices for political purposes.

One test of management's effectiveness is whether it can persuade a government to give it the freedom to set its own prices. About the only time that governments seem willing to allow managers to set prices that would maximize company profits is when the products are exported. The conclusion seems warranted that prices become a political issue when those buying the product are voters; when those buying the product are foreigners, the government is happy to let the management charge whatever the market will bear, as in private business.

PLANT LOCATION

Managers of nationalized companies like to have the freedom to build new factories and expand production facilities in areas where they perceive that costs will be lowest. Governments like to see new plants built where the political payoff will be greatest, such as areas where unemployment is high. This conflict usually is resolved simply by the government telling management what it is to do. On a few occasions management has been able to convince the government of the wisdom of its plans, and in some cases a compromise was reached. Yet the matter of plant location is clearly one which governments are not disposed to unilaterally delegate to management.

LABOR RELATIONS

Difficult problems afflict the nationalized companies in labor relations. Governments and managers both would like to minimize costs of production, yet governments must also consider the political risks. This means that governments are more inclined than the managers to give in to demands made by workers. Management is generally more inclined than are politicians to want to cut costs, get rid of unneeded workers, introduce new technology and production incentives, and lop off parts of the enterprise that are making heavy losses. Governments can only be persuaded to go along with these strategies if they feel the political costs are not too high. The manager must persuade the government that high losses carry their own political costs and that restructuring a nationalized company along efficient lines ultimately makes political and economic sense. Sir Michael Edwards at BL, Ltd. and Ian MacGregor at British Steel Corporation have had somewhat greater success in this regard than their predecessors—a testimony to their political skill.

PURCHASING

Managers like to purchase inputs from the lowest-cost source of supply, yet governments usually insist that domestic suppliers be favored over foreign suppliers. In this conflict the government can rarely be persuaded to make exceptions, even by the most charismatic and compelling manager.

NEW PRODUCTS

Should a new civil airliner be built? Should a company making aluminum ingots also make fabricated aluminum products? What kinds of new cars should be built? Such questions constantly face the managers of the nationalized companies, whose professional judgment on such issues is surely superior to that of a President, or Prime Minister, or Minister of Finance. Yet these decisions are routinely made at the highest political levels—if only because here is where the necessary finance must come. Both managers and politicians want the nationalized companies to produce products that will be commercially successful, but the government is interested in the political consequences of these decisions rather than the specific consequences to the companies involved. The management is mostly concerned with commercial growth and success, but the government must ask itself whether the political payoff from bank-rolling new products is as great as could be realized by spending the resources elsewhere.

The CEO of the nationalized company must constantly anticipate the impact of the firm's policies on the political fortunes of the government. He has only his political instincts to guide him. It is a vastly more uncertain and unpredictable environment than the regulated environment that private American firms complain about, where the manager at least has some laws and precedents for guidance. The political expectations facing the nationalized company are more constraining and more unpredictable. They depend only on the political perceptions and interests of the government in power, not on the rule of law.

FRANCE'S EXPERIMENT IN MANAGEMENT AUTONOMY

In an effort to rationalize the problem of unexpected and changing goals, creating managerial uncertainty and making planning difficult, if not impossible, the French government instituted its system of "program contracts."[1] The contract between the government and the management was to specify precisely the social and political goals the government wished the companies to achieve. These goals were to be considered costs to the firms and, in some cases, would be paid for by the government. The concept seemed highly rational and satisfactory to the managers of the French state companies. They felt it would be possible to quantify and limit the actual costs of the noneconomic goals the government was asking the firms to pursue. The great and bitter disappointment to the managers we interviewed was that after the effort to establish this eminently sensible program, it was abruptly discarded when political and economic circumstances changed. To the dismay of the managers, they were forced to return to the traditional system of sporadic and uncompensated government interference. In recent years, new attempts have been made to reinstitute program contracts in a few companies, but the managers still complain of political interference.

PROFILES OF SUCCESSFUL PUBLIC MANAGERS

While managers of state companies are often regarded by the public as inept, if not incompetent—and examples can be found to support that view—highly skilled and successful managers can be found in the public sector. "Success," of course, depends on the criteria used to judge it and these are often different for nationalized firms than for private companies. By any standard, however, three great managers stand out in the nationalized firms of Italy, France, and Great Britain since World War II: the late Enrico Mattei of the huge Italian national energy company ENI; Pierre Dreyfus, France's former Minister of Industry and former chairman of Renault; and the

Nationalized Companies

recently-retired chairman of the National Coal Board in Great Britain, Sir Derek Ezra.

A brief look at the reasons for the managerial success of these three men—in three different countries, each from a different background, and each with a different management style—reveals that all had one thing in common. Each of them cultivated a pragmatic and effective working relationship with his government. Each realized that this was crucial in order to achieve the financial support and autonomy he desired. None of them acted as if he were managing a privately owned company. The fact that they headed state-owned companies profoundly affected their style of management as well as their goals and strategies.

Enrico Mattei developed ENI (the largest Italian petro-chemical firm) into one of the most powerful economic and political forces in Italy. It was often said that he became so powerful and successful as manager that the company was run as if it were his own personal kingdom. Mattei was considered to be a master politician and a great manipulator of the press through public relations techniques. He has been likened by Dow Votaw in *The Six-Legged Dog* to Machiavelli, Cesare Borgia, the condottiere, and John D. Rockefeller, combined.[2] He may have been "ethically flexible," but his public relations skills enabled him to escape censure for acts which might have meant a ruined career for others.

Mattei had the good fortune to have operated within the "framework of weak government," in which his personality, skill, vigor, singleness of purpose, and pragmatic approach to ethics permitted him to do very much as he pleased within Italy. Indeed, his power became so great that some attribute his death in a company plane to political enemies. Persistent stories over the years attributed his great success in building ENI into a giant integrated petroleum organization, not to his acknowledged business talent, but to his mastery of Italian politics. Critics went further and accused him of bribing over half of the members of the Italian Senate and most of the top government officials.

Whether such accusations were totally correct is unimportant. The fact that ENI became one of the major economic and political forces in Italy under his management suggests he was a masterful politician as well as talented business tactician. He "knew his territory." To build a large and successful state company in Italy required a knowledge of the key points of power in Italian government and politics. Mattei was very successful in getting the permission and aid he needed to rapidly build a major integrated petroleum organization. Sheer economic prowess would not have obtained the governmental endorsement and support needed to build ENI into the giant it became so quickly. Thus, business vision was less important than political acumen in accounting for Mattei's successful career.

Pierre Dreyfus rose to international fame as manager of the French automobile company Renault after World War II. Educated in an elite French institution, he began a brilliant career in the government bureaucracy. He was Inspector General of Industry and Commerce and also held other high positions, including briefly serving as president of the state-owned coal mines (Charbonnages de France). His great success with Renault came because of his ability to keep management decisions relatively independent of government interference.

Under the Renault constitution as well as French law, the views of the company are considered in choosing a chairman, but government makes the decision. It never makes such decisions lightly, knowing that the most effective means of control is through the man appointed to head the company. Dreyfus was able to run Renault on comparatively loose reins, as nationalized companies go. This is because the French government knew him, chose him, had confidence in him, and trusted him to keep Renault on a course that would be consistent with the government's objectives.

Dreyfus' book *La Liberté de Réussir* (The Freedom to Succeed),[3] discloses fascinating details about his career and his strategies at Renault. The company's major goal was to grow—first to a position of great strength in the French market, then in the European market, and finally in the international market. The government shared this goal—it wanted to minimize imports of foreign auto manufacturers and to encourage French exports. Dreyfus was successful in coaxing the government to give him the necessary capital to steadily expand output and establish dominance in the French market and grow throughout Europe and the world. So on the basic goal of growth in the company there was agreement between Renault and the French government.

Dreyfus also persuaded the government that he was managing the company in a "tough but fair" manner, particularly with regard to labor. In negotiations with unions, Dreyfus took a strong, but not intransigent, position which inspired the confidence of the government. The fact that some of the expansion of Renault could be financed through internal generation of funds also impressed the government that Dreyfus was a careful steward of the state funds entrusted to him.

Still, the government often put pressure on Renault to do things that Dreyfus did not want to do. He proved to be a skillful negotiator in such situations. He would never give the government a flat "no," but would point out how other goals would suffer if Renault had to rescue too many companies, build plants in depressed and remote Brittany, and yet hold down prices. These conflicts were often resolved by Dreyfus talking the government into softening a proposed new control. He also knew how to avoid conflicts with the government by anticipating its views on issues. "I was never given a directive," he said when interviewed in his Paris apartment. What conflicts did arise between Dreyfus and the French government were discreetly resolved between the President, or the Minister of Finance, and Dreyfus himself. They were not allowed to become open political squabbles which threatened both the government and Dreyfus' own career.

Another factor accounting for his success, stressed by Dreyfus himself, is the French educational system. The people who become top government officials and industry leaders (including state industry executives) study at the same elite schools and know each other personally. This meant that Dreyfus was able to deal with such men as DeGaulle, Pompidou, and Giscard d'Estaing on a personal level. Conflicts could be worked out pragmatically since there was mutual trust and respect.

While Dreyfus' salary as head of Renault was set by the government salary structure at less than similar positions in the private sector, he did not hesitate to recruit able subordinate managers and pay them more than he made. His personal connections within the government made him the most powerful and flexible manager in the history of France's state-owned firms. Indeed, among managers of state industrial companies in France, his accomplishments and relative independence still remain unique.

Sir Derek Ezra was head of Britain's National Coal Board—a company that originally produced only coal, but is now an international conglomerate. Without doubt he held one of the most difficult managerial jobs in Western Europe. He astutely directed Britain's National Coal Board during the past decade, a period fraught with unprecedented political and economic problems. While the coal miners' strike destroyed the conservative Heath government and threatened to topple other governments as well, Sir Derek managed to ride out the changes. Recognizing that it was impossible to prevent government interference in the policy of the Coal Board, Sir Derek skillfully managed to convince the government to do his bidding on most issues. Furthermore, he developed new creative and profitable subsidiaries for the National Coal Board ranging from joint ventures with private companies in chemicals and hotels to special projects in Australia and China.

Sir Derek was also an effective advocate with the government for greater protection from foreign competition for the coal industry. Coal produced by the National Coal Board is substantially more expensive than imported coal from Australia and the United States. If market prices were allowed to determine who produced coal, most of the operations of the National Coal Board would have been closed long ago. Since lower wages for miners have been deemed politically infeasible, one way to ensure the survival of the industry in Britain was for the government to adopt protectionist measures. Sir Derek Ezra effectively argued for years that Britain should not close its coal mining operations simply because cheaper imports were available. This argument has persuaded governments to grant the National Coal Board a stream of new investment funds to increase productivity. He also lobbied against the increased use of foreign coal by other nationalized companies—such as the Electricity Board and British Steel Company. At the same time, he used the high price of coal produced by the National Coal Board as a way of trying to keep the miners from making extravagant wage demands, although on this matter his efforts have not always succeeded.

Like most nationalized companies, the National Coal Board seldom has shown a profit. There are good political reasons for this. The coal miners represent perhaps the most difficult group in the British economy for politicians and managers to grapple with. In fact, the National Union of Mineworkers is reputed to be headed by Marxist leaders. Any profits would tempt the coal miners to make even greater wage demands. Sir Derek adroitly finessed the frequent conflicts between the government and the workers: He kept the respect of the workers by negotiating larger wages for the miners; at the same time, he was farsighted enough to realize that productivity was the key to the future of Britain's coal mines. He diplomatically insisted on some productivity incentives to be included in the larger wage settlements. Given the generally outrageous wage demands of the National Union of Mineworkers, it is doubtful that

Nationalized Companies

anyone else could have survived so long in this job in the late 1960s and 1970s.

Sir Derek realized that his strength lay in his position between the government and the miners. The government's policies determine their wages, investment in new equipment, closures and levels of imported coal—virtually all the issues critical to the miners' well-being. While the miners depend on the government's support, the government fears the miners. The miners' ability and willingness to move the entire British economy into low gear, if not bring it to a standstill, has been dramatically demonstrated. Governments have not wished to encounter the wrath of so powerful a group. Sir Derek as a mediator managed to retain the respect of both miners and the government. He was usually able to convince both sides that he was, on balance, fair and sensible. Thus he remained, while many other managers of nationalized companies in Great Britain had come and gone.

Finally, Sir Derek's ability to raise funds from the government was little short of remarkable. Some $6 billion has been invested in modernizing the National Coal Board's operations since 1974. He raised the government's annual operating grants—the money used to balance the firm's losses—from $600 million to $1.1 billion in 1980–1981. Furthermore, the company's borrowing limit was increased from $450 million to $2 billion. Sir Derek's own persuasive powers, coupled with the government's fear of the miners, accounted for this stream of financial benefits and subsidies.

One key strategy for managing a nationalized company emerges from studying the careers of Mattei, Dreyfus, and Ezra. It is that a successful manager of the state firm must possess formidable political skills and instincts. While managers of private firms tend to place business skills foremost, the managers of nationalized companies concede that political skills are foremost in accounting for their survival. Special political sensibilities are required to maintain one's equilibrium in the face of numerous conflicting goals, whose relative importance may constantly change. Small obscure state companies that are not so politically visible and with few employees can be run closer to a private style.

The manner in which each executive worked with the government was different. Enrico Mattei was able to control the government by sheer intimidation, and perhaps by side payments as well. He succeeded in a way that no other executive to our knowledge has—by making the government afraid of him and dependent on him. A virtually incorruptible civil service ruled out this option in France. Pierre Dreyfus won his autonomy by his close personal connections and trust with government officials, and by the fact that his goal of Renault's growth paralleled the French government's goal of minimizing foreign auto imports into France. Sir Derek Ezra maintained his position as leader of the most strife-torn company in Europe by being a skilled intermediary between the government and the miners, seeking ways for both to save face.

MANAGERS WHO FAIL

Failure for the chief executive officer of a nationalized company means that he is not reappointed when he wishes to be—although it can also mean in rare cases that he is fired in the middle of a term. It is less embarrassing for both the government and the manager simply to terminate his tenure at the end of a term of appointment than it is to discharge him outright. Even failures to reappoint a CEO lead to endless speculation and analysis in the press—except when the failure to reappoint is caused by a new government that wishes to install its own team of loyal CEOs.

Aside from change-in-government "housecleanings," the single most common reason for a government to not reappoint a manager is that the manager has been a vocal critic of government policy toward the company. Disagreements are permissible, but the manager who takes his case to the public by making statements that are interpreted as criticisms or attacks on the government is destined to be fired, or not reappointed. For example, Sir Arthur Hawkins, a critic of government intervention in the Central Electricity Generating Board, who had forty-four years of experience in the electricity supply industry, had wanted to continue as chairman. But like Sir Monty Finniston, former chairman of British Steel Corporation, and British Rail's former chairman Richard Marsh, his contract was not renewed because he clashed openly with ministers and their senior civil servants.

Still, it is permissible for a chairman of a nationalized company to try to influence government policy and public opinion in favor of his company. Indeed, he is even expected to lobby and fight for its best interests. For example, Sir Peter Parker, chairman of British Rail, enjoys the image of a highly successful manager, even though his company has continually raised its prices during his tenure, while lowering many of its standards of service. Why has he been reappointed, and why was he named "Communicator of the Year" by British Association of Industrial Editors? The answer is that he has combined style and wit with vigorous campaigns to win public support for British Rail (especially support for new investment). Despite his disagreements with the Thatcher government over the amount of funding given British Rail, Sir Peter Parker has been meticulously careful to distinguish between *lobbying the government* and *criticizing the government*. He has not been drawn into public condemnations of government policy, but rather has urged that new policies be adopted. Dozens of managers who have not appreciated this distinction have lost their jobs as a result.

Another recipe for failure is the appointment of top managers in the state companies who have no experience in running a business. Although the CEO of a nationalized company must be skilled in politics, a person whose entire background is in politics and who has no acquaintance with the world of business is a high-risk candidate for a top management position in a nationalized company. The Christian Democratic party in Italy has been notorious for using its nationalized companies to reward political service. Many top managers of Italian state companies were appointed without business experience and lacked knowledge about how to run the companies they headed. Such appointments were recognized by the company employees as blatant political payoffs, and the level of morale and management effectiveness fell drastically. Political skills are foremost, but business skills cannot be ignored.

France has tended to promote highly trained technocrats within its state-owned companies. It is generally recognized that this system has been better for morale and efficiency than that adopted elsewhere in Europe. The policy of often promoting from within the ranks has given managers more incentive to work hard at their jobs and has made the French state companies perhaps the most meritocratic in Europe. By contrast it has been the usual policy in Great Britain to choose top managers for state-controlled firms from the ranks of the private sector. Often the state can only recruit managers who are in the twilight of their careers in the private sector; in fact, Sir Derek Ezra's success may be due to the fact that he was an exception to this rule. But in Great Britain, these chairmen have often chafed at the government bureaucracy, lacked political skills, and found it difficult to adopt to the subtle intrigues of political diplomacy. When they find their autonomy challenged in ways they were unaccustomed to in private business, they have often lashed out in frustration and anger. This embarrassed the government and rendered the managers politically ineffective.

By and large when the top managers of state companies have lacked either managerial experience or political acumen and leverage, they have not been successful over any stretch of time. Notable success and long tenure in heading a nationalized company are themselves exceptional. We have not been able to discover a single case of a chairman, or top executive, of a European nationalized company who was replaced for failing to earn a required rate of financial return (although the as-yet undiscovered exception which proves the rule may well exist). By contrast, there are numerous cases of chairmen and top managers who have resigned in protest, been fired, or were not reappointed because of a major disagreement with their governments over policy. If sheer survival in the job is the measure of success, the lack of political skills stands out as the single most frequent cause of failure.

THE FIGHT
FOR CONTROL

The question of who should control the giant business corporation intrigues politicians and social scientists of every academic specialty and political ideology. Americans assume the question refers to making the large privately owned corporation properly accountable to stockholders or to society. But with state firms expanding in numbers and size abroad, Western Europeans are debating who should control the giant *state-owned* company. What system of control is appropriate for such state-owned giants as France's Renault and Elf Aquitaine; Italy's IRI and ENI; Great Britain's Rolls-Royce and British Steel; Germany's Saarbergwerke and VIAG; Norway's Norsk Hydro and Aardal og Sunndal Verk; and Sweden's Statsföretag? Can the large *state-owned* corporation be made accountable to society?

Fifty years ago, socialists simply assumed that when private ownership was replaced by state ownership, the issue of accountability to society was automatically solved. Conflicts between classes and interest groups would vanish. The company would be run for the benefit of the entire society rather than for a small selfish ownership class bent on profits. Precisely who was to control the state company seemed unimportant as long as private owners were removed.

After several decades of experience with nationalized firms, such expectations seem curiously naive. State ownership has not brought about more harmonious relationships among workers, managers, consumers, suppliers, and taxpayers. Power struggles between these interest groups, previously diagnosed as a pathology of capitalism, persist in state companies and have grown more aggressive and difficult to resolve. Workers, managers, consumers, private competitors, taxpayers, and government are all inclined to perceive their individual interests as coterminous with the public interest, and they are hardly bashful about proclaiming them as such.

Who, then, should control the nationalized firm? Four general approaches to the problem are being debated in Western Europe: Government control, management control, worker control, and interest-group control. This course examines each of these systems, suggest how each would affect the policies of the state companies, and speculate on possible future developments.

GOVERNMENT CONTROL

Throughout the postwar period, the issue of control over state firms has been handled with remarkable uniformity in Western Europe, as Chapter 3 shows in detail.

Those who favor the existing system of government control say that it is necessary for political accountability to the voters. This argument is coming under increasing challenge by those who say the state companies have become autocratic, overcentralized, and accountable to no one but the government. They argue that the government uses the firms for its own political (and sometimes financial) advantage, as the Socialists argued in the 1981 French presidential election. Elected parliamentary officials further charge that the state firms are operated secretly and without effective oversight. Protracted wrangles occur over whether a parliamentary committee has the right to see memoranda and communication between the managers and government ministers. A parliamentary committee investigating British Steel in 1978 alleged that the chairman, Sir Charles Villiers, had withheld information and ordered him to deliver it to the committee. The chairman appeared before the committee "short of being sent to the Tower" and insisted on his right to refuse to supply information which he considered commercially confidential.

Another criticism of the current system of government control of state companies is that political intervention has led to poor economic performance by the state firms. Laws and public pronouncements may claim that the state firms must earn a specified return on their capital or achieve other financial objectives, but in practice these goals are rarely met. Financial targets are clearly not a major criterion governments use to judge management. Governments are not like private stockholders who insist that when management does not produce satisfactory profits, it must be replaced.

Critics of the system of government control also argue that a government has control over a formidable share of the nation's industrial assets when state ownership accounts for 20 to 50 percent of the economy. This is still something less than Stalinesque control, but it raises fears over the future of pluralism in societies with vast state holdings. The concentration of power in the hands of capitalists and business executives pales in comparison with the power a government has over the economy by control of state-owned companies. The eventual effect on Western democracies has been too little appreciated.

WORKER CONTROL

In 1976, the House of Commons in Great Britain considered a bill which would require nationalized industries' board members to be elected by workers rather than appointed by the government. The member of Parliament sponsoring the bill charged that the existing boards of the state companies were littered with captains of industry, and urged: "We need leaders who are not there because they have the approval of the Minister, but because they believe in public ownership and the democratic control of industry." After brief debate, the members of the Commons defeated the bill by a few votes. This was as close as any Western European nation has yet come to actually handing over control of the state companies to the workers.

But the idea is by no means dead. Throughout Europe there is a simmering interest among socialist parties in worker control of industry. Young middle class socialists join academic theorists to argue that the essence of socialism is worker control. The orthodox ideas on nationalization, they admit, have been found wanting. Capitalism should be replaced, they assert, but not by bureaucratic centralization. The answer is worker-controlled, perhaps worker-owned, firms. What better place to test worker control than to start by putting workers in control of state companies?

Curiously, the workers themselves appear less interested in worker control than the politicians and academics who advocate the idea. Yet these calls do reflect workers' discontent that nationalization, by itself, has not fundamentally changed their relationship to management. Workers in state firms feel as alienated from management as those in private firms, as the phrase "management exploitation" reveals.

The promise of those advocating worker control is that conflict between management and labor (or between government and labor) would be eliminated. If the managers *are* the workers (or, more precisely, if management is elected by the workers as in Yugoslavia), industrial relations would by definition be harmonious. Simply letting the workers choose their own bosses, it is argued, would remove the greatest source of conflict. At a more theoretical level, the argument is made that the large state firm is no more democratic than the large private corporation. Those most intimately involved in a corporation's policies, its workers, should have the major voice in its governance. The American political scientist Charles Lindblom reflects this emerging European socialist view when he argues that institutions that are not themselves democratically operated are less than legitimate in a democratic society.[1] The implication is that the major institutions in a state, including the state corporations, should be subject to internal democratic procedures such as voting and due process. This inclination to see "industrial democracy" as a counterpart to political democracy is illustrated by the slogan now heard throughout Europe's left-wing parties: "Now that democracies are industrialized, industry must be democratized." The place to begin, it is urged, is the state-owned companies.

One way to enhance worker power is to give workers stock in the firm, or let them purchase it at below-market prices—experiments tried in the 1960s at Renault and the state-owned National Bank of Paris. The problem with these experiments, however, has been that the workers tend to sell the shares, defeating the purpose of the plan. The goal of the programs is to give workers a share of ownership so they will find an incentive to work harder and feel they are a part owner of the company. But the Renault workers preferred to sell the stock and spend the money on consumption, or invest it in assets with greater potential for profit. The way that workers' pension funds have been invested shows that workers want to increase the value of their pension funds, not increase their ownership in generally unprofitable state enterprises. It is revealing that pension funds of many European state firms have sought a haven from socialism by investing in U.S. real estate in addition to investments which would support their own economies.

Nor are plans to give workers a share of the stock the same thing as plans to give workers *control*. Those favoring worker control are not interested in worker representation, participation, or consul-

Nationalized Companies

tation. They want a majority of workers, or worker-elected representatives, on the board of directors. Although Yugoslavia has operated along these general lines for some time, worker control in Western Europe's state firms would represent, if not a leap into darkness, at least a voyage into unchartered waters. Both the governments and managements of state firms are decidedly opposed to worker control. Governments fear losing power and control over the economy. Management fears its position under worker control could be even more chaotic and unpredictable than the present system. Thus, both governments and managers are quietly trying to distract public attention from worker control proposals and toward the concepts of consultation, participation, disclosure, and boardroom representation.

Is worker control, viewed objectively, a false hope for those who seek more efficient and less conflict-ridden state firms? The greatest danger is that the state firms would become even more conservative and unwilling to innovate. Unions in state firms have been unusually protective and defensive, demanding a silver lining in exchange for each modernization of operations. A management chosen by unions could seldom be expected to promote risk-taking and entrepreneurial creativity, or to support the search for higher productivity, the race to develop new products, the ability to penetrate new markets, or the striving to attract and reward talented people who will push the enterprise into the future. Even if worker control could work in small organizations, there is some reason to doubt that worker-controlled state firms would be flexible and competitive in large companies.

Those who speak for taxpayers and consumers frequently oppose worker control in state firms. Would worker-controlled firms pile up losses, requiring cash infusions from the government to stave off bankruptcy—as state firms do now? Would profits be reinvested, or would investment funds inevitably have to come from the state? Consumer groups protest what they say is exploitation by the indifferent, or just plain arrogant, state firms of the antimonopoly laws. The monopolistic worker-controlled firm would have little incentive to lower labor costs, so there is no reason to expect that consumers would enjoy lower prices. In Britain, the National Consumer Council has been especially critical of the efficiency and pricing policies of the nationalized companies, arguing that the nationalized industry prices have risen faster than the general rate of inflation.

MANAGEMENT CONTROL

Right-wing socialists have always wanted nationalized companies to be efficient and enterprising. No one has argued the case for efficiently managed state companies more succinctly than John Kenneth Galbraith:

> No argument against public ownership is so effective as the allegation that it is incompetent. Nothing so affirms people in mistrust of public ownership as their discovery that this is so.
>
> The solution is . . . highly professional public management. (Managers) must have extensive autonomy in decision-making, including decisions on managing and investment; this autonomy is an indispensable requirement of all effective management. Public management can never be second-guessed on decisions by the political leadership. It must be held accountable for results by the orthodox standards of cost and return. This is not a capitalist test of efficiency; it is the universal and only test.[2]

Edward Lipinske also advocates what could be called the "managerialist" position:

> Socialism means public ownership of the means of production. What we have to ensure is that the management of those public assets is in the hands of men educated at the Harvard Business School—not half educated bureaucrats in the planning ministry.[3]

Thus, the managerialist recipe for efficient state firms has three ingredients: (1). hire the best managers; (2). give them the freedom to manage; (3). firmly hold them accountable according to the traditional yardsticks of capitalism—consumer acceptance, cost control, and profit.

The managerialists have a tall order to fill. A British observer, John Elliott, wrote that a truly honest advertisement to recruit a chairman for a state company would read:

> Person willing to be pilloried in public, bullied by civil servants and Ministers in private, condemned by his employees, paid half what he could receive in the private

sector, wanted for a job which he might be allowed to keep
for three to five years. No guaranteed extras, although
good behavior should merit a knighthood if he is polite
when visiting Whitehall.[4]

Elliott's tongue-in-cheek "full disclosure ad" admirably summarizes
the formidable task of implementing the managerialist position.
Passionate arguments are raised by the European left against all
three of the managerialists' prescriptions. Politicians and unions
call on governments to appoint people of "known socialist views" to
head the state firms, not managers with training and backgrounds
in business. The problems with state companies today, they insist,
is that they have been run along excessively capitalist lines—managers are paid salaries far higher than the workers' wages; management has too much freedom to make decisions without respecting
the views of workers, consumers, parliamentarians, and the com-
munities in which the firms are located; and firms are held to cost
controls and economic goals. Critics of the managerialist position
ask the question, "What is nationalization for?"[5] Their answer is:
To change the way a firm is run and depart from capitalist policies.

Notwithstanding left-wing criticism, there have been three notable attempts to give managers, not control, but greater autonomy
to run their firms.

STATE HOLDING COMPANIES

In 1969, Sweden set up a holding company, Statsföretag, to serve
as a buffer between government and the management of state companies. Government ministers, politicians, and civil servants were
told not to interfere with individual state companies. The holding
company could insulate the subsidiaries from the political demands
and interventions that managers had complained of so loudly.[6] In
fact, the Swedes even have tried to establish the rule that any time
the state asks a state company to perform a noncommercial duty, it
must compensate the company for the cost of the additional responsibility. While accepted in theory by the government, the rule has
not always been followed in practice.

The plea of Statsföretag's chairman was that Sweden's state companies be separated into two distinct groups—those that will forever

operate at a loss and need government help, and those that can operate profitably (such as the tobacco and alcohol companies). Statsföretag says it is happy to earn profits and pay dividends from those firms that operate under normal commercial conditions, but argues that it cannot pay dividends from those companies on which the government has imposed special social obligations. For many years, the government would not agree to this plan, however, wanting commercially situated firms to subsidize the unprofitable ones rather than pay for social obligations itself. Thus, Sweden's "noble experiment" was politically difficult to implement with any consistency. Gone is the dream of 1969 when the holding company was established that the subsidiary companies could each operate profitably.

A further problem of holding companies has been that the managers of the state firms do not always want to be insulated from the government. Calling the holding company a "bureaucratic contraceptive," Sir Kenneth Keith, former chairman of Rolls-Royce, a subsidiary of Britain's state holding company, the National Enterprise Board, complained: "All our money comes via the NEB, and they puff and pant and slow the whole thing down." He finally persuaded Prime Minister Thatcher to transfer control of the company to the government directly. Although managers welcome the fact that holding companies can limit political pressures, they also want direct access to state funds.

FRANCE'S "CONTRACTS"

Another attempt to cut managers loose from political ropes that bind them began in France in 1967. A government report on the poor economic performance of French state firms recommended that political interference in state firms be restricted, if not stopped, by means of formal "contracts" negotiated between management and government.[7] The contracts were to spell out exactly what noncommercial objectives the government expected the firm to achieve. In exchange the government promised the managers the freedom to determine pricing and investment policy. The contracts were to be valid for a specified period of time, either three or five years. Contracts were signed between the government and management of some of the largest state firms—Electricité de France, S.N.C.F. (railroads), Air France, and Charbonnages de France (coal mining and chemicals). But the managers of the firms complain that the contracts have not really stopped the government from interfering in their operations. Contracts are always subject to interpretation, not by a judicial third party, but by the government itself. In some cases the government has declared that the contract ceased to be in effect because of changed circumstances (when Electricité de France's freedom to set prices was revoked). The contract approach does have the advantage of forcing the government to think a priori about its expectations of the state firms, and perhaps even required it to compensate firms for noncommercial demands (as Air France is now compensated for being forced to fly the loss-making Concordes). However, it has not given management the commercial freedom of a private-sector firm, and managers of French state firms still operate under constant surveillance and interference by representatives of government ministers.

REGULATING INTERVENTION

Europeans often debate the questions: Is it possible to subject government intervention in state industries to the rule of law? Why not simply outlaw undesirable interventions? European nationalized firms were originally set up with the belief that a distinction could be drawn between policy and implementation (or between strategy and management), the former being the prerogative of government and the latter the management's domain. The distinction, however, has proven to be impossible to maintain in day-to-day decision making. Governments have directed companies at will, claiming the matter was one of "policy" or "strategy."

There have been some attempts to spell out a clearer division of labor between government ministers and the management. The most far-reaching British proposal is that ministerial intervention should be: (1). overt, (2). in writing, (3). subject to approval by Parliament, (4). accompanied by an estimate of the extra cost expected (along with the industry's estimate if there is a disagreement), and (5). funded out of the government's own budget rather than the state firm's budget. The merit of this proposal is that it would help clarify the respective responsibilities of governments and management. If costs of noncommercial activities were quantified and met by grants-in-aid from the government, it would be far easier to assess the management's performance.

The proposal has not been adopted in any country. Governments have simply not wanted to subject themselves to such strictures and discipline. In countries whose laws require directives from governments to management be in writing, or even to be a matter of public record, politicians find ways to keep directives private. They prefer to rely on "lunch table directives," verbal instructions, or perhaps only cordial suggestions, that a policy be adopted, and resort to what a chairman of Britain's Electricity Board called "back door arm twisting." Some managers of state firms say that even if a tough law restricting intervention were passed, politicians would be resourceful in finding ways to circumvent the laws, especially if it were a politically important issue.

The managerial solution has rarely been given a chance—and is not likely to be. A system of appointing boards and managers that was totally free of political control would be necessary to free managers of state firms from political interference. Such a system would have to remove the right to select boards and managers from the government, and all other elective officials and interest groups, and place it with an independent group committed to the financial performance of the firms. Ideally, this independent group would choose managers according to the same criteria that private stockholders use with an eye to the firm's economic performance. Whether such an independent group would be politically feasible is problematic. Both the government and interest groups would oppose having a board committed to the firm's profitability. Yet, if a nation really wanted to test the hypothesis that state firms can be run as efficiently as private firms, the selection of the board and top management would need to be vested in a group committed to a commercial philosophy. But the very reluctance to discuss this alternative, coupled with the fact that this has never been tried and that, to our knowledge, no political party or interest group in Europe has even advocated such a solution, suggests that the managerialists' vision of autonomy and efficiency will remain just that—a vision.

INTEREST GROUP CONTROL

Many interest groups are affected by the policies of state firms. What role should each group have in running the firm? Which groups deserve representation on the board? How are the board members to be selected? Such questions are increasingly discussed in Europe today.

The goals and attitudes of each interest group are quite predictable. Workers press for higher incomes, shorter working hours, more job security, and better working conditions. They also favor investment that will increase productivity, as long as it does not threaten their jobs. Consumers want lower prices, better quality, better service, and favor policies that promote more competition with state firms—a goal resisted by workers and management. Private competitors of state firms want a reduction in subsidies and preferences to state firms. Suppliers want higher prices for the goods they sell to the state firms and protection from foreign competition. Management wants autonomy to run the firm, but without sacrificing the right to petition the government for financial aid and protection from foreign and domestic competition. Taxpayers want the government to stop subsidizing state firms so their taxes can be lowered. Each of these groups assert that policies which do not coincide with its interests are irresponsible, wasteful, or unfair. Each group also argues that it should have a greater voice in the governance of the firms in order to set matters straight.

To respond to these demands, several European countries now give some of these interest groups representation on boards of the state firms. France and Germany both require that four groups be represented on boards: unions (workers), consumers, government, and management. Sweden's state holding company's board includes two union leaders, management representatives, and "specialists" with business expertise. But the revealing fact about the French, German, and Swedish boards is that the government appoints the representatives of the interest groups.[8] Governments thus have succeeded in creating systems of interest group representation without actually giving up the essential lever of control—their power of appointing to the boards.

Interest groups want the right to select their own representatives to boards, but the governments have fought tenaciously to preserve their control. For example, in 1976 Britain's National Economic Development Council (NEDC) published a major study which was highly critical of past governments for continually interfering in the operation of the state firms. The solution, the report said, was a board selected by individual interest groups—with the government having only the right to approve, or disapprove, of members.[9] The British government's response to this proposal was unequivocally negative: "All appointments to boards will continue to be made by the responsible Minister." The government explained that independent boards would interrupt the "line of command between the Minister and (the) executive board which runs the industry." It justified its control by citing two facts: "The Government is the sole shareholder of the nationalized industries, and their principal banker."[10]

Two companies have experimented with giving workers the right to elect a minority of the board's directors, with the hope of improving worker morale and productivity. British Steel introduced a worker director experiment when steel was renationalized in 1967. The worker directors had three seats, a quarter of the total. After nearly ten years of experience, a study by four academics concluded:

> The worker directors had no effect on the decision making process. Management had a monopoly of knowledge, of language, and of authority: the worker directors were individuals with no sanctions and no power . . . . Nor did the scheme lead to the representation of shop floor interests at Board level or a feeling of involvement in the organization on the part of the workforce.[11]

The study suggests that the directors were political window dressing rather than an effective means of employee involvement. The goals of improving morale and productivity were not achieved at all.

A second experience with worker directors (or more precisely, union directors), began in 1978 at Britain's Post Office and lasted just two years. At the time, the appointments were announced as a significant innovation in "industrial democracy." Eric Varley, Industry Secretary, heralded the appointment of union representatives to the Post Office Board as "a challenge that was in every sense of the word an epoch-making one." The chairman of the Post Office said that he "looked forward to working with the new Board with enthusiasm." There was protracted difficulty in choosing the seven workers who were to serve on the 19-member board since all eight unions initially insisted on the right to send a representative to the board. After the argument about the distribution of union seats was finally resolved, one of the unions elected a member of the Communist party to the Board—an affiliation that momentarily troubled the government. (The issue could reappear in the future. For example, would Communists be allowed on the boards of defense firms such as British Aerospace, Dassault, and Rolls-Royce?)

Two years later, a new Industry Secretary, Sir Keith Joseph, ended the Post Office experiment. A report by a research team at Warwick University blamed management for the problems that had beset the

Nationalized Companies

board. Management withheld information from the union board members for fear of exposing their strategies to the union. Board papers were "doctored" and "censored" to suit internal politics. One manager even admitted that he "fed the board with pap."

Whether management should be "blamed" for the board's problems is debatable. The experiment may have only proved that conflicts of interest and differing perceptions between managers and unions are inevitable. It is naive to expect that managers and unions can cease to protect their own interests just because they are seated at a boardroom table rather than at a negotiating table. To expect interest groups to rise above partisan interests even denies the basic premise of those advocating interest group control of boards—that all interest groups should have the right to representation, which presumably includes the right to vigorously assert their own point of view. This is consistent with the German experience with "codetermination" boards; neither side is completely happy with having to share power. Management and labor representatives may bow to the inevitable and agree to sit together, but both sides constantly seek further changes in the law to enhance their power. The German unions point out that the present codetermination law is only a beginning, and that further changes are necessary to give them the control they seek. Similarly, union leaders in both Sweden and Holland press for control of industry.

Suppose control were actually taken away from governments and vested in interest groups—a situation that has not yet occurred in European state firms, but that has been proposed. Would the behavior of the firms change? If the firms operated at a loss, the government would be called in for financial help. If profits were not high enough to sustain an investment program, or if the money could not be raised by loans, the government's willingness to provide funds would again become critical for the firm's survival. The government would have effective control over a company that needed government revenues to survive, even if it had no formal powers over the board.

How would state firms whose boards were chosen by interest groups behave if they were somehow able to be financially independent of the government? This would depend on the balance of different interest groups represented on the board. On some issues the interests of consumers, workers, suppliers, managers, and governments coincide, but there are numerous cases where interests diverge and policy outcomes would depend upon the proportions of each group and the coalitions each would be able to form. The notion that such a board would not be the scene of continuing and even bitter debates over policy is romantic. Interest group boards are destined to be split not only on policy matters but on the degree of each group's responsibility on the board.

PERFORMANCE OF NATIONALIZED COMPANIES

How does one measure how well a company has performed or how well its top managers have achieved the goals they were instructed to accomplish? According to economic theory the way to judge the efficiency of a business firm is profitability or return on investment. Most economists would probably admit that some organizations— universities, churches, the Girl Scouts, and museums—should not be judged on how profitable they are. But these same economists would argue that aluminum and steel companies, automobile manufacturers, and hotels operate most efficiently, and thereby benefit society most, when they employ the assets of their owners profitably.

PROFIT AND LOSS

By the measure of profit and loss, the European nationalized sector is a failure. The history of nationalized companies is mostly written in red ink. When a person familiar with financial analysis scans the profit-and-loss statements of the largest European nationalized companies over the past decade, the initial reaction is disbelief and shock. How could so many huge companies lose so much so consistently? In 1980, more than half of these companies reported losses that ran into the hundreds of millions of dollars, and some over a billion dollars. More significantly, losses for many of the companies continued year after year. When "profitable," the profits were so infrequent and so small as to be almost inconsequential. Private investors would not be tempted to invest in companies with these records of performance. Of course, oil companies, both public and private, have usually been profitable in recent years. Oil companies stand out as a beacon of profitability in a sea of red ink that surrounds most state-owned companies.

We selected Europe's largest state-owned manufacturing firms because industrial or manufacturing firms are most likely to be operating in competitive markets where profits are the most widely accepted guide to operating efficiency. We list separately the state oil companies, whose pricing policies vary widely, depending on their governments' instructions. (For example, Italy's ENI has sometimes suffered large losses because of price controls, while state oil firms with greater pricing freedom have been profitable—and frequently operate as near-monopolies in their domestic markets.) State-owned companies in telephone service, electricity supply, railroads, and gas distribution were excluded because these firms tend to operate, not as commercial businesses, but as public services.

We examined the period from 1972–1981 in the profit and loss statements of the twenty-five largest state-owned industrial firms. Nine of the twenty-five firms in the sample were in private hands at the beginning of this period, yet ended the decade in the hands of the state. Thus we included their performance only for the years after they were nationalized. The profits and losses of the twenty-five firms are presented in detail in Table 1.

The central finding is the dominant pattern of losses experienced by state-owned industrial firms. In most of the ten years, the number of companies recording losses was higher than the number reporting profits. This trend toward frequent heavy losses became more pronounced as the decade progressed. Most recently, the number of loss-makers has been about double the number of profitable companies.

A second conclusion from the data is that the reported losses tend to be much larger than the reported profits. Profits in the hundreds of millions of dollars (in nine figures) were comparatively rare. It was more common for profits to be from $1 million up to $100 million (in seven or eight figures). By comparison, losses often ran up to nine or even occasionally ten figures. For example, over the ten-year period only two firms ever earned annual profits of over $250 million—British Aerospace in 1980 and SWEDYARDS in 1978. But losses of over $250 million appear twenty-six times, and occasionally reach into the billions of dollars. Even in the early years of the decade when the number of profitable firms outnumbered the loss-makers, the total losses of the few loss-makers eclipsed the total profits of the more numerous profitable firms. In 1980, for example,

Nationalized Companies

Table 1

PROFIT AND (LOSS) OF 25 LARGEST INDUSTRIAL STATE-OWNED FIRMS IN WESTERN EUROPE, 1972–1981* ($000)

	1972	1973	1974	1975	1976	1977	1978	1979	1980	1981
Aérospatiale	363	(98,942)	(76,569)	(113,816)	(129,902)	(91,045)	(19,238)	1,956	28,092	29,343
Alfa Romeo	3,677	3,677	(89,423)	(178,632)	(102,632)	(169,839)	(149,506)	(109,920)	(88,218)	(103,685)
BL (British Leyland)			(56,318)	(283,359)	61,205	(90,562)	(72,329)	(306,632)	(1,245,316)	(1,007,315)
British Aerospace						51,364	54,786	86,844	266,272	126,920
British Shipbuilders								(124,573)	(332,102)	(75,460)
British Steel	7,369	120,831	170,455	171,867	(541,209)	(164,727)	(797,597)	(600,796)	(3,891,296)	115,483
Charbonnages de France	(52,048)	(8,789)	(2,573)	(138,769)	(158,132)	(46,907)	(40,957)	(18,249)	(50,182)	(49,318)
Cockerill							(227,625)	(122,423)	(269,582)	(464,989)
Italsider	(29,056)	34,038	50,413	(110,654)	(157,609)	(446,619)	(411,236)	(309,730)	(873,700)	(1,510,775)
National Coal Board	(205,338)	(205,338)	(315,777)	-0-	11,382	47,164	36,696	(37,671)	(343,600)	(135,239)
Renault	14,800	12,902	7,261	(128,702)	122,870	4,070	2,222	241,520	160,165	(124,916)
Rolls-Royce	926	2,323	28,650	65,970	(16,538)	25,503	13,746	(133,475)	(62,789)	(6,080)
Saarbergwerke	(17,217)	(36,234)	(10,157)	(2,555)	5,059	12,100	NA	NA	2,704	31,400
Sacilor							(249,096)	(358,452)	(469,984)	(531,887)
Salzgitter		11,009	20,503	6,567	(18,517)	(40,119)	(48,272)	(1,997)	(48,668)	(175,708)
SEAT	15,083	22,869	6,463	1,085	(6,834)	5,387	(135,488)	(224,855)	(287,005)	(219,439)
SEITA		9,359		109,278	(1,581)	(32,885)	(67,218)	(55,532)	(47,445)	(22,047)
SNECMA	3,792			10,578	22,419	19,333	15,195	15,527	15,240	(24,743)
Södra Skogsägarna				4,049	4,248	(8,732)	(10,450)	(5,960)	(1,537)	NA
Statsföretag	19,025	31,561	16,869	(25,555)	44,682	(145,827)	(113,638)	45,000	29,346	(169,011)
SWEDYARDS						(414,509)	541,485	98,724	(260,212)	(56,913)
Usinor					7,782				(296,963)	(777,271)
Valmet						1,444	2,898	5,509	18,792	(38,937)
VIAG	10,680	8,971	23,684	(17,170)	16,096	14,071	(9,606)	25,325	49,290	4,210
VÖEST-Alpine	2,615	019	9,901	086	17,000	(1,500)	(23,867)	(29,124)	(65,026)	(9,356)

*Compiled from *Fortune's Annual Directory of Largest Industrial Corporations Outside the United States* and from other sources, primarily company annual reports and *Jane's Major Companies of Europe* and *Business Week's International Corporate Scoreboard*.

Table 2

PROFIT AND (LOSS) OF 25 LARGEST INDUSTRIAL PRIVATE FIRMS IN WESTERN EUROPE, 1972–1981* ($000)

	1972	1973	1974	1975	1976	1977	1978	1979	1980	1981
BASF	128,106	194,144	205,196	152,831	241,176	167,444	210,170	338,040	197,641	162,890
BAT Industries	197,775	272,213	275,735	314,041	323,541	357,987	411,061	398,940	323,247	370,903
Bayer	118,297	164,866	189,388	128,229	181,364	136,169	203,857	239,376	356,342	224,634
Ciba-Geigy	26,745	35,803	159,426	73,953	128,045	175,405	202,716	195,504	182,100	273,152
Daimler-Benz	85,993	97,527	100,496	125,768	164,182	211,010	295,054	347,794	605,149	365,212
Dunlop	9,153	42,471	19,768	(198)	68,100	NA	22,500	NA	(35,900)	(83,098)
Fiat	27,147	450	56	164	80,412	71,225	88,062	49,100	44,400	81,500
Fried. Krupp	(239)	26,275	27,444	(19,223)	10,048	NA	(10,500)	37,200	33,547	(20,858)
Générale d'Electricité	31,125	35,832	25,654	25,451	46,723	53,785	56,848	73,255	96,407	74,607
Gutehoffnungshütte	8,730	14,198	26,213	22,295	31,241	38,755	41,856	47,453	48,243	44,478
Hoechst	99,423	176,330	205,196	100,972	188,010	92,969	107,559	141,684	251,605	132,167
Imperial Chemical	229,082	449,510	567,953	424,294	442,328	394,476	577,791	880,638	(46,510)	386,983
Mannesmann	30,144	38,237	87,182	238,833	109,372	92,940	119,317	79,820	95,932	115,483
Michelin	15,425	81,419	17,322	95,164	157,140	123,658	136,976	128,540	65,813	(66,628)
Nestlé	170,759	217,783	250,093	309,365	348,922	346,633	416,131	490,865	407,785	492,604
Pechiney Ugine Kuhlmann	54,202	82,256	154,589	(37,150)	31,994	76,781	57,981	233,124	143,935	NA
Peugeot-Citroën	65,383	72,782	33,262	65,817	287,426	238,700	300,200	254,318	(348,998)	(368,825)
Philips'	233,427	323,096	273,493	152,190	212,940	258,255	327,117	308,701	165,210	143,682
Saint-Gobain	87,386	138,084	146,386	28,025	98,775	130,766	91,783	154,350	215,310	83,180
Siemens	124,694	161,897	189,149	201,275	221,969	272,971	322,021	361,938	332,434	208,157
Schneider	5,957	7,128	24,967	NA	10,706	9,829	1,044	2,422	(30,517)	(63,346)
Thomson-Brandt	26,136	48,953	34,339	38,316	43,936	42,793	53,152	65,457	72,852	(13,625)
Thyssen	15,002	61,240	201,026	99,926	105,499	65,744	61,238	87,262	61,611	(32,341)
Unilever	331,869	423,284	362,807	322,108	517,614	456,789	531,337	920,320	658,820	800,379
Rhône-Poulenc	49,073	127,328	179,556	(205,246)	(76,265)	17,094	52,872	186,019	(461,303)	(61,995)

*Compiled from *Fortune's Annual Dictionary of Largest Industrial Corporations Outside the United States* and from other sources, primarily company annual reports, *Jane's Major Companies of Europe* and *Business Week's International Corporate Scoreboard.*

Table 3
PROFIT OR (LOSS)
SALES
OF 25 LARGEST INDUSTRIAL STATE-OWNED FIRMS IN WESTERN EUROPE, 1972–1981*

	1972	1973	1974	1975	1976	1977	1978	1979	1980	1981	AVERAGE
Aérospatiale	.0005	(.1112)	(.0707)	(.0672)	(.0689)	(.0471)	(.0091)	.0007	.0090	.0096	(.0354)
Alfa Romeo	.0061	.0061	(.1162)	(.1519)	(.0941)	(.1458)	(.0921)	(.0576)	(.0387)	(.0573)	(.0741)
BL (British Leyland)			(.0154)	(.0661)	.0146	(.0199)	(.0123)	(.0483)	(.1861)	(.1732)	(.0633)
British Aerospace							.0319	.0398	.0804	.0377	.0474
British Shipbuilders								(.0792)	(.1872)	(.0359)	(.1014)
British Steel	.0020	.0282	.0319	.0322	(.1081)	(.0310)	(.1406)	(.9401)	(.5745)	.0167	(.1683)
Charbonnages de France	(.0445)	(.0058)	(.0021)	(.0623)	(.0639)	(.0196)	(.0127)	(.0041)	(.0101)	(.0115)	(.0237)
Cockerill							(.0724)	(.0376)	(.0778)	(.1185)	(.0766)
Italsider	(.0232)	.0183	.0185	(.0403)	(.0591)	(.1837)	(.1341)	(.0827)	(.2038)	(.4243)	(.1114)
National Coal Board	(.0809)	(.0809)	(.1431)	NA	.0027	.0112	.0075	(.0065)	NA	(.0138)	(.0380)
Renault	.0042	.0028	.0013	(.0164)	.0131	.0004	.0002	.0150	.0084	(.0077)	.0021
Rolls-Royce	.0009	NA	NA	NA	(.0148)	.0207	.0094	(.0742)	(.0214)	(.0021)	(.0116)
Saarbergwerke	(.0283)	(.0404)	(.0080)	(.0019)	.0033	.0081	NA	NA	.0009	NA	(.0095)
Sacilor							(.1013)	(.0952)	(.1174)	(.1608)	(.1187)
Salzgitter	NA	.0059	.0073	.0023	(.0072)	(.0148)	(.0150)	(.0005)	(.0101)	(.0413)	(.0081)
SEAT	.0282	.0293	.0080	.0011	(.0060)	.0049	(.1082)	(.0355)	(.0294)	(.0190)	(.0127)
SEITA	NA	.0169	NA	.2022	(.0027)	(.0528)	(.0905)	(.0611)	(.0449)	(.0239)	(.0071)
SNECMA	.0110	NA	NA	.0172	.0318	.0283	.0180	.0150	.0124	(.0208)	(.0141)
Södra Skogsägarna				.0089	.0074	(.0146)	(.0163)	(.0077)	(.0018)	NA	(.0040)
Statsföretag	.0204	.0245	.0093	(.0134)	.0200	(.0703)	(.0499)	.0156	.0088	(.0547)	(.0090)
SWEDYARDS						(.3970)	.6290	.0847	(.1786)	(.0403)	.0196
Usinor	.0134	.0183	.0113	(.1294)	NA	NA	NA	NA	(.0577)	(.1678)	(.0520)
Valmet	.0196	.0108	.0208	(.0148)	.0087	.0024	.0032	.0066	.0215	.0396	.0137
VIAG	.0051	.00001	.0048	.00004	.0114	.0093	(.0057)	.0108	.0183	.0017	.0082
VÖEST-Alpine					NA	NA	(.0078)	(.0073)	(.0145)	(.0022)	(.0027)
Average—All Companies	(.0044)	(.0051)	(.0161)	(.0176)	(.0181)	(.0480)	(.0077)	(.0587)	(.0664)	(.0552)	(.0367)

*Compiled from *Fortune's Annual Directory of Largest Industrial Corporations Outside the United States* and from other sources, primarily company

Table 4
PROFIT OR (LOSS)
SALES
OF 25 LARGEST INDUSTRIAL PRIVATE FIRMS IN WESTERN EUROPE, 1972–1981*

	1972	1973	1974	1975	1976	1977	1978	1979	1980	1981	AVERAGE
BASF	.0344	.0361	.0241	.0187	.0026	.0184	.0196	.0239	.0129	.0119	.0203
BAT Industries	.0769	.0729	.0535	.0511	.0484	.0541	.0530	.0421	.0294	.0259	.0507
Bayer	.0357	.0354	.0301	.0177	.0218	.0148	.0179	.0169	.0224	.0150	.0228
Ciba-Geigy	.0127	.0138	.0506	.0211	.0337	.0422	.0403	.0328	.0256	.0387	.0311
Daimler-Benz	.0207	.0176	.0319	.0359	.0432	.0508	.0244	.0233	.0354	.0224	.0306
Dunlop	.0033	.0130	.0052	(.00004)	.0163	NA	.0044	NA	(.0048)	(.0281)	.0011
Fiat	.0074	.0001	.00001	.00003	.0173	.0158	.0165	.0027	.0018	.0041	.0066
Fried. Krupp	(.0001)	.0090	.0077	(.0051)	.0026	NA	(.0018)	.0053	.0044	(.0032)	.0021
Générale d'Electricité	.0144	.0124	.0080	.0062	.0142	.0144	.0081	.0089	.0089	.0071	.0103
Gutehoffnungshütte	.0037	.0048	.0063	.0055	.0072	.0095	.0089	.0082	.0070	.0067	.0068
Hoechst	.0244	.0315	.0262	.0119	.0201	.0092	.0089	.0096	.0153	.0086	.0165
Imperial Chemical	.0541	.0847	.0095	.0616	.0592	.0485	.0664	.0773	(.0035)	.0283	.0486
Mannesmann	.0147	.0111	.0185	.0448	.0232	.0184	.0189	.0117	.0133	.0168	.0191
Michelin	.0094	.0370	.0069	.0328	.0463	.0348	.0297	.0206	.0085	(.0170)	.0209
Nestlé	.0413	.0418	.0446	.0437	.0457	.0413	.0378	.0377	.0279	.0347	.0396
Pechiney Ugine Kuhlmann	.0204	.0228	.0334	(.0085)	.0069	.0145	.0094	.0293	.0159	NA	.0160
Peugeot-Citroën	.0306	.0258	.0109	.0172	.0391	.0280	.0293	.0140	(.0207)	(.0275)	.0146
Philips'	.0376	.0398	.0290	.0142	.0185	.0203	.0216	.0186	.0090	.0084	.0217
Saint-Gobain	.0337	.0389	.0337	.0057	.0165	.0202	.0121	.0185	.0209	.0103	.0210
Siemens	.0264	.0293	.0282	.0259	.0275	.0256	.0232	.0240	.0185	.0198	.0248
Schneider	.0108	.0099	.0156	NA	.0035	.0026	.0002	.0004	(.0040)	(.0096)	.0033
Thomson-Brandt	.0172	.0243	.0149	.0131	.0124	.0107	.0105	.0093	.0084	(.0017)	.0119
Thyssen	.0049	.0144	.0232	.0114	.0133	.0079	.0067	.0064	.0040	(.0025)	.0090
Unilever	.0374	.0384	.0265	.0214	.0328	.0286	.0281	.0423	.0280	.0332	.0317
Rhône-Poulenc	.0198	.0386	.0424	(.0492)	(.0167)	.0035	.0093	.0234	(.0645)	(.0093)	(.0003)
Average—All Companies	.0237	.0281	.0232	.0165	.0222	.0232	.0201	.0211	.0044	.0080	.0192

*Compiled from *Fortune's Annual Directory of Largest Industrial Corporations Outside the United States* and from other sources, primarily company annual reports, *Jane's Major Companies of Europe* and *Business Week's International Corporate Scoreboard*.

Table 5
SALES
EMPLOYEES
OF SEVEN PAIRS OF STATE-OWNED AND PRIVATE FIRMS IN WESTERN EUROPE, 1972–1982*

	1972	1973	1974	1975	1976	1977	1978	1979	1980	1981	AVERAGE
Alfa Romeo[1]	14.58	14.58	15.89	24.68	24.35	26.05	35.93	41.46	49.78	39.98	28.73
Fiat	19.22	20.32	23.10	31.99	32.52	32.29	42.82	50.83	73.41	62.28	38.88
BL	17.02	18.75	17.54	22.37	22.78	23.34	30.74	37.64	46.68	49.68	28.65
Ford (Britain)	NA	NA	32.34	36.38	43.21	51.07	58.15	84.69	85.00	82.93	59.22
Renault	22.53	27.39	25.93	35.21	38.77	41.15	53.10	69.05	88.81	75.19	47.71
Peugeot	23.64	29.46	31.37	39.95	39.53	46.20	55.85	47.35	68.76	61.45	44.33
Salzgitter	22.56	32.89	49.68	49.92	47.73	52.40	64.11	69.50	85.15	74.64	54.81
Thyssen	33.18	46.00	57.42	61.96	57.00	62.00	70.66	87.53	100.43	87.52	66.37
Aérospatiale	16.85	21.50	26.93	46.95	53.69	57.12	63.79	79.07	90.64	86.39	55.29
Dassault[2]	28.79	52.52	49.19	63.78	81.01	76.43	90.21	107.87	156.62	146.03	85.25
Volkswagenwerk[3]	26.12	29.81	32.24	43.44	46.46	54.25	64.42	69.94	71.10	68.13	50.89
Daimler-Benz	27.75	35.59	40.61	52.68	55.56	62.38	72.33	85.66	93.29	86.26	61.21
BP	73.52	112.46	268.66	222.47	244.91	258.53	251.45	341.99	406.39	340.62	252.10
Shell	68.83	111.14	201.41	199.41	235.86	256.00	278.76	333.84	478.97	495.73	266.00

*Compiled from *Fortune's Directory of Largest Industrial Corporations Outside the United States* and from other sources, primarily company annual reports and *Jane's Major Companies of Europe.*

1. State owned firms listed first for each pair.
2. Nationalized in 1982
3. 40% state owned

total losses were $8.3 billion while total profits of the firms were $569 million.

A third result is that most firms recorded losses in more years than they recorded profits. A substantial share of firms showed losses every year, or in all but one or two years. A few firms did report profits in most years, only occasionally suffering losses—Renault and Valmet. Only British Aerospace, nationalized in 1978, recorded yearly profits, although SNECMA reported a loss only in 1981.

Thus the general pattern has been for state-owned firms to be in the red in most years and occasionally to slip into bare profitability. The high incidence of annual losses cannot be explained on the grounds that the firms were in unprofitable industries. These are the twenty-five largest state-owned manufacturing firms, producing such products as chemicals, plastics, paper products, aluminum, steel, automobiles, machine tools, machinery and fertilizers. These are products that comprise the core of modern manufacturing industry.

In contrast to state-owned firms, the twenty-five largest privately owned companies in Europe, rated by sales over the decade of 1972–1981, have sustained few losses. Only one or two companies on this list have reported consistent losses for any stretch of time. The difference appears to be that governments are willing to tolerate and subsidize losses, while private shareholders are not. Profits among these largest privately owned companies in 1981 were nearly thirteen times higher than the profits of the twenty-five largest state-owned firms, while the losses in state-owned firms were nearly eight times that of the losses sustained by the largest twenty-five privately owned companies. In 1981, admittedly a bad year for large European companies, only 17 percent of the state-owned firms reported a profit, while 65 percent of the privately owned ones did.

RETURN ON SALES

If one compares this group of twenty-five large public and twenty-five large private companies by the percentage of return (or loss) generated by their sales, a similar pattern emerges (see Tables 3 and 4). The giant state-owned industrial firms show almost universally negative returns on sales for the decade 1972–1981, while the private firms maintained generally positive returns on sales.

Nationalized companies evinced a dramatic turn for the worse after 1978. Private companies managed a positive return even in the face of a major international business downturn. For the decade, the private companies maintained on the average a slightly less than 2 percent return on sales; the state companies' average negative return on sales for the decade was nearly −4 percent.

EMPLOYEES PER $ OF SALES

What explains these wide differences in profitability? Are state-owned companies inherently less efficient? One measure of efficiency is how many employees it takes to do a job. Is overstaffing common in state-owned companies? One way to measure this is to look at the number of employees per dollar of sales. Dividing sales by employees for companies in the same industry and the same country, we find that in a small sample of seven paired firms, that in only one case—Renault v. Peugeot—did it appear that the state company was more productive than its private counterpart, but not by a wide margin. Again, private companies appear generally far more efficient than state-owned ones by the criterion of labor productivity.

RETURN ON ASSETS

Return on assets is a measure of performance that assumes that the value of assets and profits can be fairly determined. In periods of rapid inflation such as the late 1970s, it is difficult for corporations to adjust the value of their assets in order to keep their accounts realistic. The problems of depreciation of assets and reserves present are treated differently in various countries. Given these caveats about difficulty and differences in accounting methods, we can note that the spread or difference between average return on assets for the twenty-five largest state-owned and the twenty-five largest privately owned manufacturers was approximately 5 percent, in favor of the privately owned companies. Such a spread again suggests that the privately owned firms were operating more efficiently as a group than the state-owned companies. These findings are consistent with our other data. More important, perhaps, is that the state-owned companies posted a negative return on assets while the private companies reported a small positive return (see Appendix).

A COMPARISON OF THE PERFORMANCE OF MATCHED STATE-OWNED AND PRIVATELY OWNED COMPANIES

Robin Rieck, in a doctoral dissertation currently in progress at the University of Washington, matched twenty-seven pairs of state-owned and privately owned companies (by industry and country) to compare performance between 1968 and 1977.

Results from this comparative study, summarized in Table 6, suggest that state-owned companies are both less efficient and less profitable than their privately owned counterparts. The data suggest that this disparity declined slightly in the period under consideration, possibly because repeated large losses put pressure on state-owned companies to report "better results." Rieck's study ends in 1977, and more recent data indicate that the state-owned companies' losses have increased since the severe world economic downturn—as Table 1 points out.

PROFITS OVERSTATED AND LOSSES UNDERSTATED

The annual reports of nationalized companies are often more optimistic than warranted by the heavy losses they report. For a variety of reasons, profits are overstated and losses are understated in the accounts of state companies. First, profits and losses are sometimes reported before interest and taxes have been deducted, an enormous omission since interest payments are a major expense of many firms. Second, government subsidies and grants to state-owned firms, either to pay current bills or for investment, give the companies revenue that has not come from customers. To mention just one example, the National Coal Board reported profits in 1978 of nearly $37 million. Without a government grant of $172 million, the company would have reported rather high losses. Sometimes the size of grants and subsidies is made public by the government, but often it is not. It is notoriously difficult to find out the size of government grants to companies, private or state-owned—although journalists have pieced together enough clues to figure out that in France, for example, most industrial grants have gone to state-owned companies involved in high technology projects. But these disclosures still do not tell us the extent of the subsidies or the actual

Table 6
MEASURES OF PERFORMANCE OF STATE OWNED vs. PRIVATELY OWNED FIRMS IN EUROPE
(1968-1977)

	Performance Measures	Results
1.	$\dfrac{\text{Sales}}{\text{Employee}}$	Sales generated per employee lower for majority of state firms
2.	$\dfrac{\text{Adjusted Profits*}}{\text{Employees}}$	Lower for great majority of state firms
3.	$\dfrac{\text{Physical Production}}{\text{Employees}}$	Lower for majority of state firms
4.	$\dfrac{\text{Taxes Paid}}{\text{Employees}}$	Lower for majority of state firms
5.	$\dfrac{\text{Wages + Op. Exp.}}{\text{Sales}}$	Per dollar of sales, operating expenses and wages totaled higher for state firms
6.	$\dfrac{\text{Sales}}{\text{Total Assets}}$	Sales per dollar of total assets was lower for state firms
7.	$\dfrac{\text{Adjusted Output}}{\text{Total Assets}}$	Profits per dollar of total assets were much lower for state firms
8.	$\dfrac{\text{Fixed Assets}}{\text{Sales}}$	Profits over sales were lower for majority of state firms
9.	$\dfrac{\text{Adjusted Profits*}}{\text{Sales}}$	Profits over sales were lower for majority of state firms
10.	Average increase in Sales per Employee	Sales per employee has increased less on average for the state firms

*Adjusted Profits = reported profits adjusted for increase in inventory and plant and equipment produced for internal use (necessary to make profitability measure more comparable among firms and countries).

profit-or-loss performance of the companies. It appears likely that the reported figures are skewed toward profitability.

Another widely employed device is to shift costs of the nationalized firms to the government. When companies have not repaid government loans, or even interest on them, lenient governments sometimes declare the loans to be "public dividend capital." Other costs have been shifted to the government as well: redundancy and relocation payments, and even pension liabilities. Financial aid in the form of capital increases for which no dividends (or purely token dividends) are paid have also improved the financial picture reported by many nationalized companies. The habit of mixing sales revenues, government payments and subsidies, and debt write-offs makes it difficult to discover how much the state firms are in fact losing.

Do the profit-and-loss performance of the state-owned companies differ from one country to another? The common belief is that Great Britain and Italy let their state-owned companies pile up losses, but that the reins are much more tightly drawn in Germany and France. Much has been written about the French and German "gift" for running efficient state enterprises, whereas the British and Italians are said to make a mess of things. Yet the evidence suggests that these assumptions, are either exaggerated or invalid. The belief that French state companies are "run on sound business principles" does not mean that they are run profitably, as an examination of the seven French firms in Table 1 reveals. It is true that France has attempted to draw a line between the nationalized companies' commercial and political responsibilities, as described in Chapter 5. But even after any government grants for political services are included in revenues, nothing like a normal commercial return on investment is produced. The profits are typically tiny and often are swamped by losses in other years. The German firms, Salzgitter, Saarbergwerke, and VIAG have avoided huge losses, but they have not reported profits of which private firms would be proud.

In Britain, white papers pronounced in 1961, 1967, and again in 1978, that government companies should achieve a "required rate of return." But any success in achieving this has been purely accidental. Sweden and Austria have said that their state enterprises are measured by how profitable they are, but many managers continued to be promoted in the face of heavy losses throughout the decade.

Germany, France, Britain, Italy, Sweden, and Austria run their nationalized industries in some ways unique to their national traditions. But all give preeminence to political rather than market forces, and variations in this emphasis appear to us to be much smaller than is commonly believed.

Nationalized Companies

REASONS FOR LOSSES

In theory, there is no reason why state-owned firms must operate at a loss. And in practice there are indeed counter examples to the pattern. Renault's history of profits and its sales/employee ratio, for example, indicate that it is possible for state-owned companies to perform as well as, or better than, their private counterparts. But the dominant pattern of losses and lack of profitability for the state-owned sector is clear.

State-owned companies may be told to operate along commercial lines. Yet political rhetoric and management realism clash when it comes to operationalizing the proclaimed goal of profitability. Italy's IRI and ENI were organized after World War II as profit-making ventures. Their post-war caesars (especially Enrico Mattei) ran them like independent moguls. But eventually political interference entwined the firms in a spaghetti of political intrigue and infighting—and they sank deeper into losses. When Sweden's Statsföretag was established in 1970, it was told to maximize profits. For a number of years the group was somewhat profitable, due especially to Swedish Tobacco, its profitable subsidiary. But even the handsome profits of a state-owned tobacco monopoly could not continue to cover the losses of the other Statsföretag subsidiaries. In November 1982, the Swedish government withdrew the heaviest loss-making groups, such as mining, steel, and forest industries in order to administer them separately, hoping that Statsföretag can show profits in this way.[1] While this may be good public relations, it does not alter the real profit and loss situations of Sweden's state-owned companies.

A number of factors seem especially important in explaining the losses of state-owned firms. The first, and the one most frequently decried by the top executives of state-owned companies, is political interference. Per Skold came to Statsföretag with one clear instruction from the government which appointed him: Stop the losses. After a decade, he admitted that the very politicians who gave him this instruction made it impossible for him to carry it out. No matter how much politicians believe that the companies should operate profitably, conviction falls victim to politics. For example, in 1978, Prime Minister Raymond Barre of France stated: "The period of unbridled spending of public monies on enterprises whose management is unable to run them profitably is over."[2] Yet turning these industries around and stopping the subsidies is easier said than done, as Prime Minister Barre learned in the succeeding four years of his prime ministership. His success, like Thatcher's in Britain, was more rhetorical than real.

A second reason for continuing losses in many nationalized companies is that governments simply will not let vital industries go broke. No government, not even one led by Margaret Thatcher, will allow so vital an industry as steel (or automobiles or jet engines) to wither away. Thatcher, like her Labour predecessors, also has a soft spot in her heart for prestigious high technology industries, and this accounts for the continuing stream of subsidies to Rolls-Royce. If British Steel Corporation, British Leyland, and Rolls-Royce were not nationalized corporations, they would have been liquidated long ago.

The Italian government has kept afloat many loss-ridden industries—shipbuilding, steel, auto, chemicals, and fibers. Late in 1981, Italy's interministerial commission for industrial policy approved a five-year $7 billion plan to revamp the loss-ridden state steel industry. Offering a combination of fresh loans, fresh capital, and state aid, the commission said that only companies that showed promise of a profit should be funded by the government. One can only wonder whether this statement was naive or cynical. France has also been generous with grants to its state companies.

A third reason offered for losses is that some state-owned firms do not receive subsidies equal to those given by their competitors. The chairman of Austria's VÖEST has blamed the company's losses on the subsidies that other governments in Europe have given to their own steel industries.

A fourth reason is inefficiency and mismanagement. Sir Charles Villiers, former chairman of British Steel, has stated that inefficient management in the state-owned industries is insufficiently penalized. The presence of substantial private shareholders as well as the government as shareholder may make it easier to dismiss managers who have made major blunders. For example, an acting chairman of Volkswagen, a 40 percent state-owned company, resigned in 1981. At his urging, Volkswagen had purchased Triumph-Adler, an office machines manufacturer, at a time when the demand was changing to electronic office machines, and sustained heavy losses as a result. This resignation is probably explained by the fact that the majority of Volkswagen stock is not owned by the government, but is in private hands.

A fifth reason for losses is that management learns that company profits are not the real goal of the government. In fact, a government may regard other performance criteria as far more important. Aéro-spatiale, the French national airframe manufacturer, has run up losses for many years and received heavy subsidies for development programs. The company is still not making profits on Airbuses (only on missiles and defense equipment), yet it is regarded in Europe as a highly successful company because as a major exporter it saves France foreign exchange by making it unnecessary to purchase as many airplanes abroad. Similarly, the huge and continuing losses at VÖEST, Austria's largest company, do not matter as long as exports are 70 percent of sales and the company has high growth rates.

Many voters believe that state-owned firms should not earn profits of any magnitude. To many voters, politicians, and intellectuals, profits are illegitimate regardless of who owns the firm. In this view, profits of all companies, private or nationalized, are "surplus value" extracted from exploited consumers or workers. Indeed, if the state-owned firm behaved so as to maximize profits, the rationale for state ownership would come into question. Why have state ownership at all if there is no apparent difference in the behavior of state-owned and private firms? One answer is that the profits would go to the state rather than to capitalists, but this has not been persuasive to those who object to profit itself as a measure of efficiency.

This explains why both the politicians and the managers prefer the state-owned firm to break even or incur losses. That profits are the best measure of efficiency is recognized by most economists, including socialists, but this is not widely understood by the consumers and workers who make up the electorate. Profit maximization for most state-owned firms is not politically feasible.

Managers have discovered that profits can create more problems than they solve. Profits incite labor to demand higher wages. Profits also cause government ministers to ask the firm to pursue new social goals, such as hiring more workers, lowering prices, buying from noncompetitive domestic sources, rescuing failing firms, and aiding in regional development by building new plants in areas of high unemployment. The manager of the state-owned firm has no incentive to maximize profits.

The view that governments should support state-owned firms which fail to earn a market-level return on investment goes to the heart of the debate over the role of nationalized companies in a nation's economy. This debate was well illustrated in 1981 when Sir Keith Joseph was questioned in the House of Commons as he announced further production cut-backs and disposals of assets to cut the losses of British Steel Corporation. Sir Keith Joseph stated: "The taxpayer has already contributed £4,000 million to British Steel Corporation over the past five years. A further £450 million is being made available in the current year and now we are being asked to consider yet further calls on the taxpayer." John Silken, the Labour spokesman, was unimpressed by this argument and demanded: "Are you in favor of a British bulk steel company or not?" "Yes, if it could be profitable," Sir Keith Joseph retorted. Another Labour M.P. pressed, "Do you ever think about the social cost?" Sir Keith concluded that the £5 billion contributed by taxpayers to the industry was an important measure of the social cost.[3]

Who was right, Sir Keith Joseph, who thought that British Steel should be run like a private business, or the Labour M.P.s who felt that the company's losses were not as important as the social costs if the company failed? There is little political agreement on this "Chrysler" question. Few state-owned companies can pretend to have paid their way in any real sense, yet those who defend them insist that the benefits to their national economies exceed the economic costs they have extracted from those economies.

This debate reveals the single most important reason for the losses of most nationalized companies. The inability to generate customer revenues that exceed the ever mounting costs these firms are asked to shoulder predestines the company to loss. It is really in no one's interest—not the government's, or management's, or the workers'—to minimize these firms' costs. The political appeal of pursuing social goals rather than the purely economic goal of profit is so strong that state-owned companies, even if they do operate profitably (escape losses) in some years, are not profit maximizers.

ADDENDUM: THE PROFITABLE FEW

One group of large state-owned firms in Western Europe has consistently earned profits of some magnitude: British Petroleum, Dutch State Mines, Elf-Aquitaine, and Norsk Hydro. These profitable firms are in the petroleum or natural gas industries.

Nationalized Companies

Two facts about that industry explain why state-owned oil firms are usually able to operate profitably (see Table 7). First, because many tend to export most of their output, less political pressure is put on the firms to lower prices. (While governments minimize consumption of petroleum for balance of payments reasons, there is political opposition to raising prices to domestic consumers of petroleum products.) Second, the industry hires comparatively few workers, so the firms are not subject to pressures to raise labor costs as much as many other industries. There is simply no formidable political constituency which will suffer if the state-owned oil and natural gas firms earn substantial profits.

The fact that state-owned oil firms often operate profitably does not suggest, however, that they place the same emphasis on profitability as private oil firms. Indeed, comparative data suggest that state-owned oil firms are not profit maximizers. Governments are often content to have the state-owned oil firms supply the domestic economy with oil. How profitably that job is done appears to be secondary.

A second class of profitable state-owned firms consists of monopolies, nationalized to produce revenues for the government budget. Salt, tobacco, matches, and alcoholic beverages are the usual examples. The earliest French government enterprise, SEITA, the tobacco and matches company, was organized by Napoleon in 1811 as a revenue producer and run as a branch of the national treasury. Japan and Sweden have done the same with their state-owned tobacco monopolies. Even in the United States, where there is little tradition of nationalized business, many states own retail liquor stores which raise revenues for their treasuries. State ownership of highly profitable monopolies can reduce taxes, which has obvious political appeal.

The third class of firms which may be profitable are public utilities or regulated industries with monopolies or dominant market power so that competition does not determine prices. In these industries— postal service, urban transport, telecommunications, electricity, gas, railways, and bus service—there is an unresolvable debate over what criteria should be used to measure efficiency. One view is that the firms' performance should be measured by a broad set of economic and social criteria. The other belief is that financial targets such as return on assets should be the primary gauge. The profit-and-loss performance of these firms has varied widely from year to year.

Table 7

PROFIT AND (LOSS) OF TEN LARGEST EUROPEAN STATE-OWNED OIL COMPANIES*
($000)

	1972	1973	1974	1975	1976	1977	1978	1979	1980	1981
British Petroleum	175,813	760,539	1,140,117	369,202	324,615	530,797	853,057	3,439,582	3,337,121	2,063,272
DSM	34,864	50,838	192,995	56,935	49,980	44,961	11,809	44,446	12,542	40,488
Elf Aquitaine	11,300	103,891	238,229	119,875	340,108	358,974	332,336	1,310,132	1,378,222	632,316
ENI	17,646	64,982	(91,256)	(134,869)	(37,026)	(249,391)	(367,892)	89,040	98,046	383,234
ENPETROL				20,221	19,909	15,986	18,451	25,226	17,233	22,690
Neste		5,838	3,056	(8,994)	(2,574)	4,314	4,825	30,560	29,608	14,258
Norsk Hydro				11,635	66,661	30,088	13,652	28,985	79,442	71,698
ÖMV	130,588	2,397	13,153	3,902	8,301	8,110	16,555	19,616	17,641	8,248
Statoil									41,128	178,050
Veba Oil	(6,398)	17,557	12,118	(24,333)	(7,359)	(50,980)	25,872	50,367	35,975	32,113

*Compiled from *Fortune's Annual Directory of Largest Industrial Corporations Outside the United States* and from other sources, primarily company annual reports and *Jane's Major Companies of Europe*.

Appendix 1 to Chapter 6
PROFIT OR (LOSS)
ASSETS
OF 25 LARGEST INDUSTRIAL STATE-OWNED FIRMS IN WESTERN EUROPE, 1972–1981*

	1972	1973	1974	1975	1976	1977	1978	1979	1980	1981	AVERAGE
Aérospatiale	.0002	NA	(.0303)	(.0385)	(.0451)	(.0283)	(.0051)	.0004	.0057	.0060	(.0150)
Alfa Romeo	.0029	.0029	(.0524)	(.1058)	(.0771)	(.1085)	(.0843)	(.0600)	(.0346)	(.0423)	(.0559)
BL (British Leyland)			(.0220)	(.1207)	.0223	(.0249)	(.0164)	(.0586)	(.2195)	(.2354)	(.0844)
British Aerospace						.0487	.0379	.0455	.0869	.0414	.0521
British Shipbuilders								(.1169)	(.3022)	(.0609)	(.1600)
British Steel	.0021	.0339	.0267	.0274	(.0866)	(.0225)	(.0875)	(.0557)	(.5248)	.0151	(.0672)
Charbonnages de France	(.0280)	(.0040)	(.0014)	(.0533)	(.0606)	(.0154)	(.0083)	(.0035)	(.0097)	(.0102)	(.0194)
Cockerill							(.0589)	(.0312)	(.0777)	(.1098)	(.0694)
Italsider	(.0069)	.0070	.0097	(.0193)	(.0275)	(.0703)	(.0557)	(.0421)	(.1214)	(.1960)	(.0522)
National Coal Board	(.1600)	(.1597)	(.2348)	NA	.0047	.0171	.0093	(.0069)	.0086	(.0141)	(.0680)
Renault	.0092	.0071	.0033	(.0480)	NA	.0005	.0002	NA	NA	(.0105)	(.0033)
Rolls-Royce	.0045	NA	NA	NA	(.0173)	.0229	.0103	(.0730)	(.0212)	(.0023)	(.0109)
Saarbergwerke	(.0258)	(.0419)	(.0095)	(.0024)	.0040	.0081	NA	NA	.0013	NA	(.0094)
Sacilor	NA	NA	NA	NA	NA		(.0482)	(.0563)	(.0844)	(.1048)	(.0734)
Salzgitter	NA	.0041	.0078	.0026	(.0063)	(.0129)	(.0133)	(.0004)	(.0102)	(.0433)	(.0080)
SEAT	.0218	.0255	.0049	.0014	(.0090)	.0061	(.1128)	(.1184)	(.1260)	(.1040)	(.0410)
SEITA				.1338	(.0019)	(.0322)	(.0522)	(.0390)	(.0326)	(.0202)	(.0063)
SNECMA	.0072	NA	NA	.0103	.0210	.0153	.0088	.0078	.0070	(.0112)	.0083
Södra Skogsägarna				.0077	.0057	(.0121)	(.0126)	(.0059)	(.0016)	NA	(.0031)
Statsföretag	.0112	.0156	.0058	NA	.0101	(.0387)	(.0278)	.0097	.0063	(.0404)	(.0053)
SWEDYARDS							.1444	.0194	(.0624)	(.0163)	(.0117)
Usinor						(.1437)			(.0395)	(.1062)	(.0728)
Valmet					.0093	.0017	.0027	.0051	.0135	(.0277)	.0008
VIAG	.0099	.0067	.0150	(.0113)	.0092	.0070	(.0042)	.0088	.0181	.0015	.0061
VÖEST-Alpine	.0036	.00001	.0037	.00003	NA	NA	(.0047)	(.0049)	(.0115)	(.0017)	(.0019)
Average—All Companies	(.0106)	(.0086)	(.0195)	(.0144)	(.0144)	(.0191)	(.0172)	(.0262)	(.0638)	(.0475)	(.0308)

*Compiled from Fortune's Annual Directory of Largest Industrial Corporations Outside the United States and from other sources, primarily company annual reports and Jane's Major Companies of Europe and Business Week's International Corporate Scoreboard.

Appendix 2 to Chapter 6
PROFIT OR (LOSS)
ASSETS
OF 25 LARGEST INDUSTRIAL PRIVATE FIRMS IN WESTERN EUROPE, 1972–1981*

	1972	1973	1974	1975	1976	1977	1978	1979	1980	1981	AVERAGE
BASF	.0265	.0401	.0338	.0269	.0366	.0229	.0241	.0335	.0213	.0183	.0284
BAT Industries	.0682	.0660	.0612	.0661	.0624	.0614	.0580	.0444	.0376	.0388	.0564
Bayer	.0288	.0328	.0278	.0172	.0213	.0135	.0167	.0173	.0265	.0175	.0219
Ciba-Geigy	.0101	.0095	.0316	.0137	.0218	.0245	.0236	.0187	.0184	.0307	.0203
Daimler-Benz	.0531	.0451	.0385	.0462	.0460	.0471	.0417	.0425	.0683	.0400	.0468
Dunlop	.0033	.0134	.0056	(.0001)	NA	NA	NA	NA	NA	NA	.0055
Fiat	.0101	.0001	.00001	.00003	.0130	.0155	.0154	NA	NA	NA	.0077
Fried. Krupp	(.0001)	.0130	.0103	(.0077)	.0035	NA	(.0022)	.0071	.0068	(.0044)	.0029
Générale d'Electricité	.0103	.0094	.0056	.0050	.0121	.0110	.0096	.0106	.0074	.0062	.0087
Gutehoffnungshütte	.0047	.0056	.0098	.0067	.0094	.0103	.0092	.0090	.0081	.0089	.0082
Hoechst	.0214	.0300	.0263	.0130	.0215	.0094	.0094	.0111	.0204	.0113	.0176
Imperial Chemical	.0417	.0698	.0764	.0592	.0569	.0435	.0548	.0687	(.0032)	.0276	.0495
Mannesmann	.0183	.0193	.0330	.0717	.0290	.0223	.0257	.0150	.0196	.0240	.0278
Michelin	.0576	.0422	.0354	.0244	.0386	.0265	.0225	.0169	.0078	(.0079)	.0264
Nestlé	.0523	.0569	.0490	.0600	.0611	.0466	.0457	.0480	.0403	.0495	.0509
Pechiney Ugine Kuhlmann	.0139	.0181	.0276	(.0068)	.0058	.0127	.0080	.0285	.0191	NA	.0141
Peugeot-Citroën	.0431	.0400	.0095	.0261	.0596	.0385	.0340	.0207	(.0300)	(.0369)	.0209
Philips'	.0340	.0377	.0242	.0136	.0174	.0188	.0201	.0167	.0089	.0082	.0200
Saint-Gobain	.0277	.0346	.0285	.0055	.0174	.0206	.0119	.0192	.0231	.0120	.0200
Siemens	.0292	.0262	.0303	.0291	.0270	.0244	.0216	.0213	.0187	.0142	.0242
Schneider	.0476	.0470	.1360	NA	.0016	.0010	.0001	.0002	(.0021)	(.0061)	.0250
Thomson-Brandt	.0156	.0242	.0130	.0114	.0114	.0085	.0083	.0080	.0083	(.0017)	.0107
Thyssen	.0060	.0171	.0386	.0204	.0187	.0115	.0087	.0088	.0065	(.0041)	.0132
Unilever	.0710	.0756	.0510	.0462	.0664	.0504	.0478	.0745	.0498	.0638	.0596
Rhône-Poulenc	.0147	.0302	.0327	(.0391)	(.0154)	.0032	.0084	.0238	(.0707)	(.0105)	(.0023)
Average—All Companies	.0284	.0321	.0334	.0212	.0268	.0226	.0218	.0245	.0134	.0136	.0237

*Compiled from Fortune's Annual Directory of Largest Industrial Corporations Outside the United States and from other sources, primarily company annual reports and Jane's Major Companies of Europe and Business Week's International Corporate Scoreboard.

Nationalized Companies

The decision to operate public utilities profitably or at a loss is a quintessentially political decision, about which successive governments have differed—and not necessarily along predictable lines. In Great Britain the conservative Heath government was committed to fight inflation by, among other things, keeping down the prices of the services of the nationalized industries, choosing to subsidize the firms' heavy losses out of the government budget. The subsequent Wilson and Callaghan governments adopted a different approach toward the firms, giving them greater pricing freedom and expecting them to break even, if not earn a small profit.

In France, too, government expectations of state-owned public utilities have varied. For many years, France maintained the prices of certain state-produced services at artifically low levels. Since the nationalized industries provide many services which are part of the cost-of-living index, their price increases had a "multiplier effect" on the price level of the entire economy as many labor contracts specify that wages be tied to the cost-of-living index. The French had thought that the government subsidy of the losses of the state-owned public utilities could avert more serious wage-induced inflation. Yet in the wake of the 1978 elections Prime Minister Barre instructed state-owned public utilities to balance their budgets and operate on a break-even basis. The political damage to the government of President Giscard d'Estaing from the resulting price increases was considerable.

A fourth category of profitable state-owned enterprise can occasionally be found buried within the large state-owned conglomerates which operate numerous divisions or product lines. For example, Renault's foreign exchange operations have been reported to be highly profitable. Elf's pharmaceuticals division has been profitable, as has Compower, one of Britain's largest computer services companies, wholly owned by the National Coal Board. BA Helicopters and British Air Tours, subsidiaries of British Airways, also operate in the black. Profits of these sectors appear to be well hidden within the large enterprises, and their low visibility makes it possible to operate along these lines.

But as a rule profits are only acceptable if they are comparatively modest, or if they are profits earned primarily from exports, and not at the expense of domestic customers or workers, or if the firm is a monopoly, nationalized to create revenues for the government. Where at least one of these conditions does not exist, profitability for the state-owned firm is simply not in the interests of the government.

THE CHALLENGE TO ECONOMIC THEORY

It appears that the standard economic theories of profit maximization do not accurately describe the great bulk of state companies. The extension of state ownership to more and more sectors of industry poses a challenge to the economics profession to develop new theories that account for the behavior of the state firm. These theories are likely to be grounded as much in politics as in economics.

CHAPTER
SEVEN

IS THE
NATIONALIZED
COMPANY UNFAIR
COMPETITION?

Why should private companies observe the rules of free trade when a growing number of their competitors are protected from the rigors of competition by government subsidies and preferential treatment? More and more owners of private corporations are asking this question as government ownership of business expands in Europe and throughout the world. Private companies find it increasingly difficult to compete against state-owned firms that are not required to earn profits and that receive direct and indirect subsidies.

Although foreign state-owned companies have not in the past posed a serious competitive challenge, the spread of state ownership during the 1970s is rapidly changing the rules of the game on international competition. William Sneath, chairman of Union Carbide, predicted that, by the mid-1980s, companies owned or controlled by governments would account for nearly 50 percent of the U.S. chemical industry's competition in export markets in such important sectors as petrochemicals, fertilizers, and plastics. He concluded that this spread of government ownership is contributing to the further erosion of America's share of chemical export markets.

William T. Seawell, chairman of Pan Am, noted that many foreign flag airlines are government-owned, and virtually all are government-financed, or otherwise aided. In congressional hearings on world steel trade, William H. Knoell, chief executive officer of Cyclops Corporation, stated that 55 percent of the noncommunist world steel production is owned outright by government and that the trend is toward more government ownership.

Although European Economic Community officials have a strong mandate to enforce fair competition, the EEC is fighting a rearguard action against most European nations' policies of nationalization and subsidization. The EEC has been especially reluctant to take effective action against uncompetitive practices of state enterprises, knowing that such action would receive a hostile reception in member nations. It is one thing for the EEC to charge private companies with anticompetitive behavior; it is quite another to bring action against governments themselves. The *Financial Times* of London declared: "The European Commission's attempt to tackle state aids to publicly owned industry has foundered almost totally upon the rocks of political, technical, and legal difficulties."[1]

Behind the discussion about the future role of nationalized companies in international trade and investment lie two competing theories of political economics. One is the conventional economic wisdom of free trade espoused by most economists. A second nationalistic theory of international trade relies on conscious, but sub rosa, protection of many domestic markets and promotion of exports in selected industries. A brief look at each view follows.

FREE TRADE: THE CONVENTIONAL WISDOM

Statesmen and economists who advocate free trade as the optimal policy for governments to pursue believe that it is the most efficient way to allocate the world's resources. In an economy that does not trade, domestic consumption is limited to what is produced internally. With international trade, it is possible for a nation to increase its consumption of goods by producing those goods in which it has a comparative advantage. If each nation produces the products it can make most efficiently and then trades with other nations, total welfare is enhanced.

Adam Smith, the earliest and best-known economist to spell out the advantages of free trade, opposed the mercantilistic practices of governments in the eighteenth century. He argued that they encouraged a government to define a nation's wealth, or well-being, by the amount of precious metals, such as gold, that it held. A country would export more than it imported to increase the inflow of precious metals. Governments used tariffs and export subsidies to create, or maintain, a favorable balance of trade. Smith pointed out correctly that the wealth of a nation was determined by the standard of living of its citizens, not by the amount of gold a government might hoard. The classical economists argued, therefore, that tariffs and export subsidies which could increase a government's stock of gold might also reduce the economy's standard of living. The population of a nation was better off if it had a larger number of consumption alternatives and if government opened up markets which would maximize the consumer's opportunities.

As Melvyn Krauss has pointed out, this classical argument for free trade is really based on a preference for public interest over special interest. "Free trade is best for the overall economy, even though individual groups may lose from this policy."[2] It can be argued that while certain groups, including the government, could gain from the imposition of tariffs, artificial barriers, and export subsidies, the overall welfare of the population would be decreased.

There is clearly a good deal of common sense and realism behind classical free trade theory. The advantages to the consumer of competition among an array of foreign and domestic products does not have to be proven. But the determination of maximum consumer welfare becomes more ticklish when one poses the question: Is it in a nation's interests to be a unilateral free trader, *i.e.*, to let in another nation's exports without discrimination even though the exporting nation closes its markets to imports? Is free trade a one-way street? Hard-core free traders would say it is. If some governments wish to subsidize their exports and deny others access to their markets, they are foolishly reducing their efficiency and harming their own consumers. The laugh is on them, not on the employees in the free market nation who have been laid off because of subsidized foreign competition.

But others remain unconvinced that unilateral free trade is in a nation's interests. If it is clearly advantageous to have open markets, why have Europe and Japan raised new barriers as old ones have been lowered? Has the Japanese practice of using every restriction and prohibitive practice imaginable to bar foreign products and investment been counterproductive for Japan's standard of living and damaging to their international competitiveness? In fact, Japanese consumers *have* suffered by being effectively denied many foreign products. Yet the Japanese have used extensive protection to build up their own industries into formidable exporting machines, and their per capita growth of income has clearly outpaced that of the other industrial nations.

In short, criticism of the pure theory of free trade is twofold: It is based on idealizations that do not describe the real world. Second, no nation (not even the United States) seems to have become internationally competitive by opening up its industries competition from nations with more advanced industries. Precisely the opposite policy—careful nurturing and protection of industry—has been followed in successful growth economies.

MODERN INDUSTRIAL POLICY AND NATIONALIZATION: THREAT TO FREE TRADE

The major trading partners of the United States today follow policies of direct intervention in industry and careful protection of their domestic markets. Although a succession of trade treaties have been signed, and international trade has continued to grow in the postwar period, the tariffs that the treaties reduced have been supplanted by explicit state aids to industry and invisible protection and subsidy of domestic industries. Growth in international trade has slowed appreciably, leading to uncertainty over its future. American consumers have generally been the beneficiaries of free trade, but with more and more industries facing subsidized competition from abroad, it is not surprising that citizens should begin to wonder whether free trade is still in the nation's interest. Other nations benefit from trade far more than the U.S. consumer, whose life would not change appreciably if denied products from subsidized and protected foreign firms.

Unilateral free trade violates our notions of legal reciprocity—that two parties to a contract should follow generally similar rules. The system of free trade that has developed so successfully since World War II has been based on a set of rules (treaties) which specify that firms are generally not to be subsidized by the state and that markets will be increasingly opened by all parties.

We contend that the growth of nationalization makes nations profoundly more protectionist, at the same time that it makes them more anxious to export. Thus, nationalization has the dual effect of protecting a nation's markets from foreign competition and putting many nationalized firms under special pressure to earn foreign exchange by aggressively exporting. Political goals replace the traditional profit-maximizing goal of the firm. In the light of these developments, nations that believe in private business must ask: Should we assume a posture of unilateral free trade toward the protectionist practices of nationalized industries? The neoclassical theory of free trade might argue that we should not treat others as we are treated, but should keep our markets open. The second view is that existing trade laws should be vigorously enforced and greatly strengthened vis-à-vis nationalized industries so that private firms are not operating at a disadvantage.

ARE STATE-OWNED FIRMS UNSUBSIDIZED COMPETITORS?

In comparison with their privately owned competitors, state-owned companies have distinct advantages which they often use to maximize exports and minimize imports. We will consider several of the protectionist policies nationalized companies follow.

NO NEED TO EARN PROFITS

The biggest advantage for state-owned companies is their ability to succeed, and even thrive, without earning profits. Even an inefficient company can be a formidable competitor when it is subsidized and its deficits are covered by the government.

United States Treasury Department data show that in 1977 the British Steel Corporation, whose production facilities were acknowledged to be old, overstaffed, and inefficient, was underselling efficient Japanese steelmakers on the west coast of the United States. Since British Steel's losses in 1977 alone were over $800 million, the decision to sell steel at such low prices was interpreted as a political decision to maintain employment rather than a commercial one. In July 1978, the British government requested new aid of $930 million for British Steel.

U.S. trade policy has long recognized that state companies in the Communist nations do not live by profit and loss statements. One well-known example is the Soviet merchant marine, which entered the world market by setting prices up to 40 percent below all competition. Its economic mandate was to earn foreign exchange (although another mission may have been strategic), and it did not need worry about operating profitably. Prices were set to win a large market share.

In some cases, state-owned firms are even expanding into new markets abroad as they lose money. Governments have been covering losses of some firms for over ten years. Such major firms as Salzgitter, Aérospatiale, Rolls-Royce, and IRI continue to be propped up by their governments despite stunning and continuing losses. Both socialist and "free market" governments continue to pour money into both fledgling and long-standing industries to help them compete in world markets, or to keep out foreign sales in their home markets. By defying capitalist rules of survival in the marketplace, they are increasingly a major factor in the international competitive equation.

PREFERENTIAL ACCESS TO STATE FINANCING

State-owned companies enjoy ready access to the state purse. Their top executives meet regularly with the finance minister to discuss cash and investment needs. When private banks provide loans to state companies, the government usually guarantees repayment, ensuring a low interest rate.

The annual state budgets in many European countries provide for major financial assistance to state-owned companies. Sometimes the aid is for immediate cash needs (as in the case of much recent assistance to British Leyland (now BL, Ltd.), British Steel, and some other state-owned companies), but more often funds are set aside for investment projects. Competition in export financing has become a preoccupation in many countries. When the TriStar was fitted with British-made Rolls-Royce engines, the British government agreed to finance both the planes and the engines for Pan American in order to ensure the engine contract for Rolls-Royce. Thus, government-financed investment is based more on such political consideration as maintaining employment and exports than on considerations of profitability. State companies can readily adopt "political" investment criteria without risking their futures, whereas private corporations that ignore profitability will not survive.

In Italy, the state has granted IRI interest-free capital grants and subsidized loans. A leading Italian scholar, Pasquale Saracento, notes that state firms in Italy "can obtain financial resources the state may supply practically without limit"—as long as they are earmarked for politically appealing "social purposes,"[3] but subsidies earmarked for a social goal like retraining workers could actually be used to subsidize exports. In recent years, politicians have forced the Italian state-owned banks, under their strong protests, to grant

Nationalized Companies

financial aid to state concerns that faced bankruptcy. Through a series of capital writedowns, the Italian state has subsidized state firms and allowed them to continue to operate, despite huge losses.

The Japanese have pioneered a technique which includes subsidizing not only their own companies but foreign state firms to acquire new technology. Japanese companies and Britain's Rolls-Royce have teamed up to develop a jet aircraft engine. The Japanese government pledged 75 percent of the funding for the project, estimated at $655 million. The Dutch government has over the years supplied generous grants for Volvo Car (40 percent state-owned). The Norwegian government announced plans to spend $140 million from 1980 to 1985 to subsidize production and finance of Norsk Jernverk, the state's iron and steel producer, which suffers heavy losses. The Norwegian government pointed out that essentially all the European governments are playing the same game, so they are setting no precedent.

One of the most heavily subsidized state enterprises in Europe is the development and expansion in production and marketing of the airliner Airbus. The governments of three countries (France, West Germany, and Britain) have bankrolled the operation at all critical stages. The Airbus Consortium is made up of the state-owned aerospace companies of Britain, France, Spain, and of West Germany's minority state-owned company.

In France, the government regularly supplies capital grants to state enterprises at below-market interest rates. Although the scope of such aid is kept secret, a report by the French Economy Ministry revealed that much of French aid to industry goes to eight companies. Half of these are government-owned, or government-controlled through a blocking minority interest, including Aérospatiale, Charbonnages de France, the French Atomic Energy Commission, and Dassault. Hervé Hannoun, the Inspector of Finances who made the study, alleged that state assistance had become an integral part of these companies' profit-and-loss structure and frequently amounted to more than their real reported earnings. In some cases, the aid—such as the funds which support research in electronics and government-assisted contracts abroad—had become a permanent fixture of the companies' operations. Hannoun's report called for pressure on the companies to increase their underlying profitability and demonstrate the effectiveness of the aid. But the Economy Ministry's conclusion to the report rejected a profitability requirement, claiming that aid policy is based on factors other than profit.

The list of examples of preferential financing could be vastly extended. In Japan, Japan Air Lines raises money "cheaply and easily on the domestic capital market by issuing paper with a government guarantee,"[4] a privilege not available to privately owned Japanese airline companies. Although European governments are increasing their aid to private businesses as well, their favored beneficiaries are their own enterprises. As a result, the number and size of grants and subsidized loans to state firms well exceeds those given to private firms.

BUILT-IN MARKETS

Governments usually encourage state-owned companies to give preference to domestic sources in their purchasing. Although this practice is, with a few exceptions, a direct violation of trade laws, examples of direct government influence in procurement decisions of state-owned enterprises abound. As more companies come under state ownership, governments acquire power to influence, or control, purchasing decisions in large sectors of the economy.

For example, when managers of two major European state-owned airlines—Air France and British Airways—announced their preference for U.S.-manufactured airplanes, the political repercussions were instantaneous. The French government persuaded the management of Air France to agree to a compromise by which the company would purchase most of its planes from the French state-owned aerospace firm Aérospatiale. The announced preference of the British Airways deputy chairman for a United States-made plane was followed by calls in Parliament for his immediate dismissal.

Governments themselves are the largest purchasers of goods and services in every major country today. They represent a growing share of world trade and are involved in purchasing practically every kind of good and service, ranging from computers, automobiles, and office machines to every type of military equipment. Bids for this vast amount of business are in many cases not open to foreign competitors. U.S. companies are complaining that the huge Japanese state-owned company, Nippon Telegraph and Telephone Corp., bought from foreign U.S. manufacturers only on a token basis.

When governments became major owners of computer companies, they assured these businesses of a healthy number of orders from state agencies. Government campaigns to encourage the public to purchase domestic products require a government to buy domestic

Nationalized Companies

products itself, and the pressure is doubly compelling when a state-owned enterprise makes the product.

Public opinion runs strongly against having governments purchase from foreign companies. In the case of British Airways, a British aerospace union adopted a resolution demanding that the nationalized aerospace industry be given preference on all future contracts. Private companies sometimes join the unions in vociferously opposing foreign purchases by state-owned companies. For example, private paper producing companies in Britain recently called on the government to instruct all the nationalized companies to purchase domestic paper products.

The number of major government purchases of foreign products is tiny. One of the best-known is the United States Coast Guard's purchase of $214.8 million worth of helicopters from Aérospatiale, the French state-owned aerospace concern. The company's bid was $1.1 million lower than that of Bell Helicopter, a division of Textron. Foreigners were delighted at this sign of a newly opened market in the United States since it marked a departure from that country's purchasing practices and was unlike what a European government would have done. The day that the French government buys foreign helicopters rather than those of its domestic supplier will be the day the President of France serves California wine at state dinners.

Laws to put government procurement (and purchases by government companies) on a competitive basis have been expanded as a result of the Tokyo Round reforms, to be sure. These laws are unlikely to change the purchasing practices of government enterprises. An indication of the continuing reluctance of foreign governments to purchase according to competitive specifications was demonstrated by West Germany as recently as late 1980. The West German government reversed an official procurement decision of the state of Bremen, which had ordered a $5.5 million American-made computer, and gave the contract to a West German company. The West German Minister of Research and Technology threatened to cut off the subsidy to Bremen that would cover 85 percent of the cost of the computer. And despite the free trade philosophy espoused by the Thatcher government in Britain, it was just not politically possible for her to allow Britain's Inland Revenue Service to purchase IBM computers. The bid went to the domestic producer, ICL, which was having more than its share of difficulties in maintaining orders.

Regardless of the logical appeal of abstract principles of free trade,

public opinion is much more strongly opposed to government purchases of foreign goods than to individual or private purchases. In
the case of a state-owned company, the unpopular decision to "buy
foreign" is seen by voters as the government's responsibility. Governments must find ways to finesse new trade rules on public procurement so they can continue their policies of buying domestic. A
large, state-owned sector enormously expands the scope of public
procurement, and thereby multiplies the protectionist forces in the
entire economy.

MONOPOLY POWER

Governments have often chosen to nationalize entire industries
by placing competing businesses under single state ownership. Great
Britain is particularly known for this strategy. Companies such as
British Steel, British Aerospace, the National Coal Board, and British Shipbuilders have a dominant position in their respective industries. Even though this policy has encouraged monopoly, these
companies still have had difficulty achieving financial health. Subsidies and grants from the state have often been necessary to protect
these domestic monopolies from foreign competition.

The most glaring case of the granting of monopolies to a major
state-owned industry is the airlines. With the sole exception of the
United States and Switzerland, the major nations of the world have
state-owned international airlines. The firms are often explicitly
chartered to pursue a range of objectives other than profit. These
goals include acquiring foreign exchange, aiding national defense,
encouraging tourism, and maintaining employment.

When such firms as Aeritalia, Air France, Air India, Sabena, and
British Airways suffer immense losses—as they have in many years—
there is no question about their future ability to operate. Not one
major foreign state-owned airline has dropped out of the industry.
Their government owners see to that.

Direct subsidies and other contract preferences are ways to support state monopolies; other arrangements to insulate them from
competition are also possible. State-owned airlines often control the
reservations system, travel agents, remuneration, tour wholesalers,
and freight forwarders, and use that control to maximize market
share. Such control has reached its apex in the Soviet Union; European and other state-owned airlines enjoy monopolistic advan-

tages to varying degrees. United States airlines, in contrast, are forbidden by antitrust law from having any control over travel agents, tour wholesalers, or freight forwarders. As anyone who has traveled by air within Europe knows, air travelers on popular routes pay exorbitant prices to subsidize the unprofitable activities of the state airlines.

State-owned monopolies which raise revenues for the state treasury—alcoholic beverages, tobacco, salt, and matches for example—are typically insulated from competition. A state-owned monopoly that purchases products in a competitive world market and is the sole seller in an inelastic domestic market can generally return substantial profits to the state treasury. This is a formidable barrier to trade, and imports will be reduced below the free trade competitive level. This result has encouraged, not deterred, governments from using this mechanism wherever they are allowed to do so.

The issue is far more complex than revenue-maximizing. Where some of the sales are generated overseas and some produced domestically—as in the case of Japanese tobacco and alcohol monopolies—the state-owned seller favors domestic producers and even pays higher prices to them. Revenue for the government is not maximized by such a policy, but the protectionist impact of the state monopolist is thus maximized. M. M. Kostecki reports that state monopolies for tobacco and alcoholic beverages impose mark-ups on imported products 40 to 60 percent higher than those on domestic output.[5] Thus, state monopolies are concerned with the two goals of raising revenues and protecting local markets.

OPERATING WITHOUT FEAR OF BANKRUPTCY

Just as state-owned companies need not earn profits to prosper, neither do their losses lead to bankruptcy. Judging by the evidence, state ownership usually confers immortality on an enterprise. Governments rarely allow their companies to go bankrupt, regardless of how staggering their losses may be. In fact, large losses are as likely to be followed by massive new injections of investment funds as by cutbacks in production, as the Italian state-owned enterprises have shown. Despite large losses, Italian state-owned steel companies have added to capacity, in violation of EEC directives; and Italian state-owned textile companies that have been reporting losses for ten years or more still live to compete another day. France's

Aérospatiale has lost money in most of the past ten years; Rolls-Royce has a similar record. Yet because the companies are considered important parts of the industrial mix of their respective countries, their survival is assured.

The European state steel industries are often said to be in danger of closing, unless their operations become more efficient and, at least, break even financially. The British government has warned that new legislation will give it the right to liquidate British Steel if it continues to lose money. The management of Italsider has threatened to close down the company, which employs 40,000 workers, unless the government provides more money. Only a naive person would be fooled by these threats. When governments are faced with the prospects of mass unemployment from liquidating industrial firms, they find it far easier politically to provide another billion dollars in aid. Keeping the life-support systems going is cheaper than the total cost of corporate euthanasia, at least in the short run.

But it is a curious concession to free market ideology that governments feel compelled to accompany announcements of new cash infusions with stern warnings that this is the "last time" such funds will be available. They say the funds are to allow the companies to restructure and become competitive. The management issues a statement saying that its corporate plan shows it becoming profitable in three to five years. The onus is now on the workers to show that they can become truly efficient and competitive, the government says. Only one thing is more predictable than this rhetoric. It is that the management will be back for more cash in a year or two.

SUBSIDIZATION OF DOMESTIC INDUSTRY

State-owned companies sometimes subsidize other domestic industry. Governments often use state-owned companies to assist domestic corporations by, for example, selling goods or services at lower than cost. The price of state-supplied coal has been subsidized for many years in France (as shown by the consistent losses of Charbonnages de France), benefitting coal users.

State-owned banks are called on to give special support to exporting companies. Maurice Lauré, chairman of state-owned Société Générale (one of the large French banks), said that the banks "are absolutely in the front rank" in their aid to French exports. Two

Nationalized Companies

state-owned banks have lent the loss-ridden French steel industry most of the $6 billion it has received in loans. Considering that banks in France are state-owned, the implications become clear.

The Swedish government has used the purchasing power of state-owned companies to avoid layoffs in the private sector. When the large Swedish telecommunications business, L. M. Ericsson Co., threatened to close some of its operations, the government gave its telephone company an extra $70 million to place additional orders for new equipment from Ericsson.

Revenues from state-owned natural resources can go directly to subsidize domestic industry. In the debate on what to do with the revenues of the state-owned British National Oil Corporation (which controls North Sea oil operations), some British political sentiment had been to use the oil money to "revitalize" British industry. No one appeared to object to such a subsidy on the grounds that it would be anticompetitive. Even though Britain's National Coal Board had received large subsidies for years, some large purchasers of coal found it cheaper to buy imported coal than British coal. To reduce coal imports, the Thatcher government announced special price reductions for National Coal Board coal sold to British Steel Corporation and the Central Electricity Generating Board, both state-owned firms with their own financial problems. That these price concessions promise to add to the Coal Board's deficit did not seem to be a major stumbling block. However, the price concessions only extended to the two state-owned purchasers and did not apply to private businesses purchasing coal. Governments use state firms to subsidize other state firms, even giving preference to state firms over private firms when this seems politically wise. In the British example, protectionism seems to take precedence over ideology.

The chain of cross subsidization becomes more complex when one examines the state electricity companies. All European governments subsidize industry by providing cheap electricity to industrial users. In fact, it is impossible to learn the terms of power-supply contracts. To note one case, the price at which British Aluminium is supplied electricity has not been disclosed, although it was set low to allow British Aluminium to manufacture at an internationally competitive price. Similar examples have come to light in Germany and France, but ferreting out the details is almost impossible. This may suggest that the amount of the subsidy is embarrassingly high.

Many oil producing nations today are remarkably open about their intentions to use oil revenues to assist other industries. Norway's government is concerned about the growing domination of the oil and gas industry in its economy, and the problems created for other industries by the strength of the nation's currency. One proposal being discussed is to use oil revenues to supply companies with risk capital. They could use this to buy ownership stakes in foreign companies which had the products, production technology, and market expertise to develop production in Norway. Mexico has been totally unabashed about using oil revenues to negotiate government-to-government package deals which require foreign companies to build manufacturing plants in Mexico; so have the Mideast oil producing countries. Oil and minerals increasingly are being used as a basis for industrial diversification, into downstream petrochemical processing and manufacturing.

Cross-subsidization can become so elaborate that it really amounts to a "package deal" involving state and private firms. T. Ozawa describes "Japan's New Resource Diplomacy," in which a consortium of Japanese firms combines with the government to take on what the Japanese government calls a "national project."

> Once an overseas venture is designated as a "national project," government aid takes the form of participation by the Overseas Economic Cooperation Fund (OECF), Japan's official aid agency, as the major stockholder of a Japanese investment company set up by the consortium involved in such a project. The Japanese government also provides low-interest loans both to the Japanese partner and to the host government from the Export-Import Bank of Japan, loans often to be used as equity capital from both parties.[6]

Japanese industry locates developing countries where natural resources are available, and proposes a package of economic aid from government-owned agencies. Four parties are involved in such agreements: Japanese industry, the Japanese government, the government of the host country, and a foreign firm (usually state-owned). Ozawa concludes:

> As long as the project has a long-term economic significance for the supply of industrial resources, the Japanese government sooner or later comes to the aid of Japanese industry. . . .The Japanese government channels funds

Nationalized Companies

> through the Export-Import Bank of Japan and the OECF,
> the latter becoming the major shareholder of the Japanese
> investment company set up for a particular project.[7]

Japan has been the most successful developer of these large package deals, combining commitments of business and government on both sides. Europeans have, however, shown a growing aptitude for engineering such long-term contracts. Finnish, German, Austrian, and Italian state-owned firms do a lot of business with the communist-bloc countries. Most of these ventures (again, typically resources-for-technology and capital goods) involve governments as a vital part of the bargaining unit. The details of the contracts are rarely made public, so we have only the most general notions about the transactions. The only clue is that state firms appear to be used by the European governments in a noncommercial way (perhaps to preserve détente, support the local currency, and provide jobs). The governments themselves promise to purchase products from Eastern Europe in the exchange. The firms most involved in these contracts—Austria's VÖEST, Italy's ENI, West Germany's Saarbergwerke and Salzgitter, and Finland's Valmet—continue to operate at a loss year after year. This suggests that their behavior cannot be described as commercially motivated. To understand the rationale behind the contracts requires an understanding of the promises made not only by the state-owned firms but also by their government owners.

How important are these "package deals" and "new resources diplomacy" in international trade? Kostecki's conclusion is that they account for "a huge portion of international trade in resource commodities."[8] As he says, "as a consequence, there is a relatively small international free market for these commodities." Kostecki even asserts that Canada, France, and Japan set up international development agencies which are presented as government bodies managing development aid, but are, in fact, nationalized trading companies.

JOINT ACTIONS TO RESTRAIN COMPETITION

On April 2, 1980, several leading French and German steel manufacturers were found guilty of price-fixing and market sharing by the European Commission, and were fined $1.5 million. European antitrust law, like that of the United States, holds that joint actions by competitors to affect price or output levels are illegal. In the United States, such actions are "per se" violations of the antitrust laws—illegal regardless of any apparent "reasonableness" that the guilty parties may seek to establish.

The irony is that the European Commission itself operates a huge quota and price-fixing cartel for the steel industry, started as the Davignon Plan in 1977. The EEC-orchestrated cartel in steel allowed each nation's steel industry to survive in the recession-prone economy of the late 1970s. The EEC can set up its own cartel for an industry, but it does not approve of steel companies trying to improve on it by their own private cartels. "Such illegitimate regulation of the market by producers who make their own rules is tantamount to usurpation of the Commission's powers," the Commission press release said. Community-sponsored "recession cartels" are permissible, but private cartels are not.

It is no coincidence that "recession cartels" should be found in industries heavily populated by state firms, such as steel. Europe's state-owned steel firms have been especially keen to form an EEC-sponsored cartel to cut back production, while private firms have resisted. Private firms are forced to make cutbacks in production rather early as costs rise or as markets contract, but state firms need not operate in such haste. Governments are reluctant to lay off workers, and there will be much political rhetoric and controversy prior to taking any action. Furthermore, governments do not trust other government firms to shrink their industries either. The only way that excess capacity can be reduced is if all agree to mutually negotiated cutbacks.

This is more easily said than done. The German government, for example, initially showed little enthusiasm for the EEC plan to cut output because Germany has one of Europe's more efficient steel industries; British Steel Corporation's chairman Ian MacGregor then warned that if Germany did not go along, British Steel would retaliate against low-priced West German steel by offering even lower prices to German customers. British Steel contended that much of the steel reaching British markets was subsidized by the German government. On this point, MacGregor was on solid ground. In fact, German regional government officials, wanting to maintain high employment levels in their regions, have a variety of industrial-aid schemes. The West German steel industry also receives assistance indirectly through federal assistance to the railways, which follow

Nationalized Companies

a buy-national policy in steel purchases. Of course, the Germans would be just as correct in pointing out that British Steel threatened to surpass all records for losing money and for subsidization. Rather than having all sides stop the subsidies, restoring the normal ground rules of competition, the easiest solution is to first point fingers at each other's sins of subsidization and then form a government-sanctioned cartel. To the EEC's "common agricultural policy," effective in keeping foreign agricultural products out of the EEC countries, has now been added a "common steel policy," and calls for a united EEC stand against automobile imports are being heard from all countries. Firms in trouble are finding that the EEC can be a forum for discussing the common problems of ailing industries, but that joint actions can be taken to control prices output and imports.

Consider also the following circumstance: A huge domestic market exists for an ubiquitous consumer product. The government has a monopoly on production, but not sales, of the product, since consumers are buying more and more foreign-made products. To stem the tide, a group of government companies get together and decide to launch a new joint product. Each monopoly will manufacture the common brand name under agreed specifications. One might expect that such an action would be held illegal under even the weakest antitrust laws. But such is not the case. The situation referred to is the jointly launched announcement by five state-owned tobacco monopolies in France, Japan, Austria, Italy, and Portugal of a new cigarette named "Champagne."

The brand is targeted to compete with leading United States and British brands in Western Europe and Japan. It should be pointed out that both countries have increased their market share in Western Europe and Japan in recent years. That growth has been achieved at the expense of the domestic state-owned producers. France and Italy's tobacco monopolies have reported losses in recent years, while the other state monopolists have been profitable, but "sleepy," according to the editor of the trade publication, *World Tobacco*.

Should similar joint ventures be undertaken by private competitors threatened by foreign competition? What would public reaction be if General Motors, Ford, and Chrysler announced joint production and marketing of a car to keep out foreign competition? If private firms are not allowed to proceed in this manner, why should state-owned companies be able to band together to fight foreign imports? In France, Italy, Austria or Japan it was simply assumed that such action was legal if it meant that the state-owned domestic producer gained a larger market share.

HIDDEN SUBSIDIES

Subsidies to corporations are more easily disguised than are tariffs or quotas. It is nearly impossible to unravel the tangled financial relations between governments and state enterprises. Japan, for example, has many types of state-owned "public corporations" which are used to subsidize national economic endeavors. A new study notes that most areas of technological expertise in which Japan is preeminent—shipbuilding, railroads, steel, electronics, cameras— were developed by mixed public and private enterprises, or under official auspices.[9]

A lack of consistent accounting standards has made it especially easy for governments to hide subsidies to state-owned businesses. Not only do different companies adopt widely differing accounting practices, but these practices often change from year to year. Thus, it is next to impossible to know how performance is being measured, or what the company's true goals are. This chaotic situation moved *The Economist* to proclaim: "Shoot the nationalized auditors—no one would notice."[10]

The EEC has been struggling to correct the problem it calls "transparency"—government money and policies that benefit a state-owned enterprise, but are difficult to trace and measure. For example, is a government cash grant really going for new plant and equipment, or will it subsidize the price of a product in foreign markets? The EEC treaty states that the same rules of competition apply to state as to private companies, but by the EEC's own admission, attempts to attack state aid to state-owned companies have met with little success. The problem is not that governments are unaware of the anticompetitive impact of such subsidies, but that they zealously guard their right to set national economic policy.

U.S. POLICY OPTIONS

In an age of proliferating subsidies to foreign state-owned and private firms, bold and unequivocal action is necessary to prevent further erosion of private markets at home and abroad. One possi-

Nationalized Companies

bility is that the U.S. could grant the same kind of protection and subsidies to its private firms, challenging the nations which increasingly use state enterprises to protect their national and export markets. Reliance on enforcement of the GATT rules seems less likely to prove effective; the effort could drag on for years and would be subject to political whims and international pressures.

United States trade policy could consider imports from state-owned and subsidized companies on the same basis as those from centrally-controlled economies. Trade with state-owned enterprises poses essentially the same problems in policy as does trade with the Communist nations, because the firms are instruments of national economic policy. Trade policy should acknowledge that state-owned companies that do not make the same level of return on investment as their private counterparts are in fact subsidized.

It is time to recognize that while other nations talk about free trade, they have in fact moved toward veiled, but active, protectionism. The United States government urgently needs a special office with exclusive responsibility for studying and monitoring the changing scope, behavior, and competitive impact of state-owned companies abroad.

NATIONALIZED COMPANIES: A BALANCE SHEET

A comparison of nationalized firms and privately owned firms reveals that it is not the diversity but the similarities among state firms that really catch the eye. Nationalized firms have their differences, but they bear a strong family likeness to each other. This we found to be true throughout Western Europe. Our purpose in this chapter is to summarize those similarities among state firms that we have observed, especially those features which distinguish them from private firms.

MANAGERIAL COMPARISONS

FLEXIBILITY

The top managers of state-owned firms do not have the same degree of freedom, or control over the firm, as managers of private companies. State firms tend to lack the ability to make a dynamic response that a highly competitive firm has. The nationalized company is inclined to be conservative, inefficient, and less disposed to take risks. It can be argued, of course, that these are the characteristics of large, bureaucratic organizations. However, most government, or state-owned firms, are unable to overcome these problems, while their counterparts in the private sector have a compelling need to do so if they are to survive in a competitive world. Managers of state-owned firms have less power to hire or fire, to choose their own managerial team, to instill a certain *esprit de corps*, to move rapidly in and out of markets, or to close or sell off outmoded or obsolete plants. The top manager of a state firm, therefore, has less effective power to influence how the enterprise functions. The manager's creative ideas must often be "sold" to the government in power if they are to be implemented. This in itself is a drain on the manager's energy and time and checks the initiative and managerial competence of the state-owned firm.

PRODUCT INNOVATION

Science and technology are no respecters of tradition. The capacity of state-owned firms to adapt to new conditions and to develop innovative products and plans will be severely tested in the years ahead. If the past is prologue, technologies that meet new consumer needs are not likely to arise in the state sector. One is hard pressed to find many examples of nationalized firms in Western Europe which have earned reputations for product innovation and general alertness to consumer needs and interests. Especially with state monopolies, haughty indifference to consumers is par for the course.

The communications revolution in the next twenty years will be an excellent test of innovative capacity. The traditional post office and telephone industries will change dramatically as some traditional services shrink and new services expand. Will the state-owned monopolies be the lowest cost producers of these services? Or will the private telecommunications companies (such as AT&T, IBM, Xerox, and ITT) come up with the most important innovations? Texas Instruments recently announced that for five cents it could send messages anywhere in the world on a satellite network system. This may be an indication of which sector to bet on for innovation.

Nonetheless the monopoly position of state-owned companies in many countries has tended to prevent private innovations from being established as rapidly, or as inexpensively, as possible. It is increasingly likely that the postal services, both in the United States and Europe, could be handled more effectively by a completely private system. Whether that could ever come about is highly doubtful given the political power of the postal unions. Even in the United States, where the managers of the postal system have attempted to achieve a style of operation resembling private management, they have been constrained by Congress. The entrenched unions, allied with the subsidized users of "junk mail," fight the proponents of lower cost technologies developed in the private sector. Probably compromises will be reached through which the European state-owned telecommunications systems will, of necessity, adopt the new innovations, but be burdened with overstaffing by their strong unions.

INCENTIVES, STAFFING AND LABOR COSTS

When a top executive of a state-owned company makes a mistake in picking staff and subordinates, it is often difficult, if not impossible, to correct it. The protection for workers in state firms makes it difficult to eliminate inefficient, unproductive, and lazy workers. In contrast, the private firm and the private CEO have somewhat greater power over personnel matters. The young executive who performs dramatically in his job can be leapfrogged up the promotion ladder and receive big bonuses to keep him in the company. The private company can build a system to recognize especially good people and reward them. This is more difficult in European state-owned firms. A storm has arisen over the allegedly high salaries paid to some top managers of state firms, even when these salaries are a fraction of what top managers earn in private companies. Thus, the twin problems of lack of incentives to reward the most able workers and managers and the difficulty of eliminating unneeded, or incompetent, or inefficient staff continually plague the bureaucracies in state-owned firms. Despite legislation making it increasingly difficult for private firms to eliminate overstaffing, they still have the advantage of providing incentives.

There do not seem to be substantial differences in wage costs between state-owned and privately owned companies. But in work rules, pension schemes, and other conditions of employment, state-owned companies are often more generous. Because state firms have sometimes managed to pass on some of these costs (especially the funding for pension funds), to the general state budget, their true labor costs are often understated.

The past decade has witnessed important wage disputes between governments and unions in the state-owned firms in nearly all European nations. State firms have experienced industrial unrest on an unprecedented scale, especially in Britain and Italy. In the British case, the post office disputes in 1971, the miners' strikes in 1972 and 1974 were all explicit confrontations between the unions and the conservative government. Labor disputes in the nationalized companies appear to be between management and the unions, but the real players are the government (which holds the public purse) and the unions.

Wages can adjust more easily to market clearing levels where unions are not so strong. But in the state-owned sector uniform rates of compensation are most strongly ingrained, and it is difficult if not impossible to vary compensation according to supply and demand. This state of affairs often leads to a confrontation between monopoly unions and a monopoly employer, with the minister of finance the banker of last resort.

FINANCE AND INVESTMENT

The state-owned company tends to obtain money for new investment from the government, not from the capital markets. Its investment policies reflect a wide range of social and political goals, rather than profitability.

Counter-cyclical investment policies for state companies are especially favored by governments. The nationalized banks in France were told by the Mitterrand government to loan money to the newly nationalized companies to update their plant and equipment, in order to stimulate the economy. The chairman of a state-owned firm is, among other things, a fundraiser, soliciting the money from the government in power. Maintaining an effective relationship with the prime minister, or finance minister, is an essential, if unwritten, part of the job description for the CEO of a publicly owned company. An effective advocate for the firm can coax subsidies, low interest loans, or capital write-offs for a variety of purposes: employing people in economically depressed areas, subsidizing the pension fund, pollution abatement, carrying inventories, new product development, new plant construction, or even meeting short-term cash needs.

A case in point is Airbus Industrie, a consortium of state-owned and state-subsidized companies whose development costs are paid by several governments in Western Europe. The decision about what planes should be built is made not by management but by the member governments themselves, because the governments must pay for development of the new planes. The private capital markets were sufficiently dubious about the project—after the Concorde fiasco— that the only way money could be raised was directly through government grants in aid.

ECONOMIC PERFORMANCE

PROFITS, LOSSES AND SUBSIDIES

The financial data on state-owned companies for the past decade reveal persistent and heavy financial losses, even though governments and managers of the state firms use a variety of accounting tricks to understate them. Why do governments and voters tolerate the heavy drain on public funds that these staggering losses entail? Perhaps one can understand that a government on humanitarian grounds would provide "alimony" for brief periods of time to help a company get back on its feet. But there are many state companies coming to the government year in and year out, seeking new funds for every need, ranging from investment in foreign assets to paying next week's wages. It is difficult to understand and explain governments' tolerance for such fiscal extravagance.

The reason for governments' generosity is partly a credit to shrewd managers who promise that they can see the "light at the end of the tunnel." Skillful managers such as BL's Sir Michael Edwards can keep a company afloat indefinitely. In BL's case, this was achieved even when, in 1980, losses ran at a level of $1,500 per car sold—a formidable job of salesmanship. A chairman must promise the public that better times lie ahead, that government money will help the company become competitive, and that to liquidate would cost the government vastly more money in severance pay and in losses to subcontractors and suppliers than continuing in business. The arguments have considerable appeal, but they reflect a considerable departure from the market process of efficient replacing inefficient uses of capital. Further, the arguments emphasize short-run political versus long-run economic considerations.

Governments do not relish this strain on their budgets, but do not know what to do in the face of continuing losses. They are reluctant to shut down basic industries, when the industries are prestigious or fundamental, to the economy, as in the case of aerospace, steel, computers, and automobiles. It is tantamount to a national admission of failure for a major nation to proclaim that it can no longer compete in a basic industry. When a failing firm is already nationalized, the government can either cut it back and/or give it more money.

State firms are not the only declining industries, as the United

Nationalized Companies

States has learned in the last decade, but there are still major differences of degree between government response to economic failure in the United States and Western Europe. The U.S. economy is still much less heavily subsidized and protected than European countries or Japan—despite claims to the contrary by foreign trade ministers. U.S. Steel and the American automobile firms have problems, but because they are not state-owned (except for American Motors, which is controlled by the French government) they are not as direct a government responsibility. The United States government has not become as involved in rescuing companies as its European counterparts. Governments of Western Europe will go to almost any length to help companies survive, including numerous devices to protect failing industries from foreign competition.

Investments initially promoted to the public as guaranteeing quick turn-arounds have a way of becoming a drain on the national budget. The leading French steel firm, Usinor, was effectively nationalized in 1978 because of its tremendous losses. The French adopted a tough policy of mandatory layoffs and 30,000 jobs were trimmed. The goal was to quickly restore the company to health. But recent reports show that the end of subsidies is nowhere in sight.

One of the most perplexing characteristics of state companies is the fact that large losses can often be consistent with high rates of growth. In April 1981, Salzgitter, the German state steel company, announced that its 1980 losses would be "very high," but also revealed that capital spending for the year had totaled 339,000,000 Deutschemarks, an increase of 60 percent over the previous year. The investment in Salzgitter, a perennial loss-maker, is seen as a continuing subsidy to a company that is kept afloat despite its losses. A similar pattern can be detected in many other state firms. Losses do not lead to a shrinking of plant and sales but to a reinfusion of cash from the state. Subsidies, by their very nature, tend to flow toward problems rather than opportunities, especially when companies are subsidized for extended periods. Managers and markets quickly become addicted to subsidies, and it requires a strong politician to cut the flow.

The casual attitude toward cost consciousness on the part of managers of nationalized firms is not a personal failing. It is not that the managers are inherently, or necessarily, inefficient, or do not want to operate efficiently. Failure to minimize costs is generally the result of government, not management, policies. The problem is the failure of governments to adopt the profit criterion for measuring top management's performance. Inefficiency brings only displeasure, not retrenchment or elimination of management.

PROTECTIONISM

Protectionism is in itself a form of subsidy to a firm, as it insulates the firm from lower cost producers abroad. State firms are protected by an array of protectionist policies as we have shown in Chapter 7. Individual companies find it difficult to compete with governments—especially on the soil of foreign governments.

A company that is assured of the bulk of sales in a nation can succumb to the temptation of becoming inefficient. Poor products, inefficiently produced—the twin signs of poor management—would lead to disaster if the floodgates of international competition were opened. It is easier for a government to control domestic competition, as the French and Italian governments have done in protecting their state auto companies, Renault and Alfa Romeo. Although major privately owned domestic competitors exist in both nations (Peugeot and Fiat), both nations have clamped far stricter limits on foreign imports (Japanese auto especially) than the United States has. One could plausibly conclude that BL's unfavorable market share has been partially due to the fact of the British government's more liberal position toward auto imports.

MONOPOLY

Monopoly is a further cause of high costs in state-owned industries. Firms with monopoly power find it easy to raise prices or reduce the quality of services. There is ample evidence that this has been done, especially in the case of state-owned companies producing services— post offices, airlines, railroads, telephone companies, and natural gas producers. In competitive industries, skimping on quality can lead to a fall in market share, but a state monopoly is largely insulated from such realities.

One of the justifications for French nationalization is the desire to create "national champions," state-owned and state-sanctioned monopolies that can keep foreign competitors at bay and carry the nation's export burden. The French notion is that today economies of scale require only a single firm in many industries and that the state should own monopolies. Regardless of the relative efficiency of publicly owned or privately owned monopolies, nationalization is not the only way to harness monopoly power and create industrial champions for the nation.

POLITICAL ENVIRONMENT

THE "BOTTOM LINE"

In the state firm there is a bottom line, but it is political, not financial. The successful state-owned firm is one that has persuaded the government and the public that it is successful—like a politician. The goals of maintaining employment, buying national rather than foreign products, exporting, investing in depressed areas, and investing in new technology are all politically accepted as legitimate goals for a firm. The manager of a state company is not measured by how much profit his company makes, but rather by how well he gets along with the government and how well he seems to be achieving public goals.

The private company's constant awareness of the need to operate profitably stands in bold relief. The manager of a private company is charged with finding ways of increasing profits. Financial responsibility focuses the manager's mind on two essential issues: new ways of expanding revenue and new ways of controlling costs to achieve profits. But in the state firm, the twin problems of expanding revenues and reducing costs are nowhere as urgent.

INTEREST GROUPS

Managers of state-owned firms constantly find themselves constrained in their decisions or policy making by the political power of interest groups. While interest groups can bring suits and lobby governments against private firms, they have more leverage against state firms. After all, major decisions by the state firm require the acquiescence of the Minister of Finance.

The power of the interest groups lies in their ability to raise questions in parliament and the press and to embarrass the government by attacking its policies toward the firms. The veto effects of smaller political interest groups, therefore, may be enhanced when dealing with state-owned firms. When a decision is finally made, political opponents may challenge both the management and the government. Planning and decision making in nationalized companies, therefore, tends to be somewhat more reactive than in the private sector, and management has less freedom to cut costs—even if it has the incentives to do so.

The importance of interest group politics in the state firm's decision making is well described by Franco Grassini, a former official in an Italian state enterprise. In order for an upwardly mobile employee to rise in the company bureaucracy, Grassini notes the employee needs "a certain willingness to accept requests from the political world." Managers "should never dismiss anybody. . . . A political request to create new jobs has also played a role. . . . Once a new factory has to be built, the location is very important from a political point of view."[1] Once an employee has achieved a top position, the same expectations remain.

REGULATION AND CONTROL

From some governments' point of view, an advantage of nationalization over private ownership is that governments need not enact formal regulatory laws, or set up elaborate enforcement mechanisms, in order to affect company behavior. They can give instructions directly or indirectly to the managers of the nationalized firms. The detailed regulatory approach, so highly developed in the United States, frames laws to address issues of social cost across the board, and makes all firms responsible for taking similar actions to solve similar problems. Leaving regulation up to politicians who sporadically instruct state companies to behave in certain ways creates a comparatively unstable environment. Managers of state firms wonder what the current priorities really are, or what they will be in six months.

Government regulation of the private sector has increasingly narrowed the difference in performance between state-owned and privately owned firms. In recent years, it has made the private firm less flexible and enhanced the power of interest groups in corporate actions. In the United States, and to a degree in Great Britain, these trends have been reversed somewhat in the last few years by conservative governments. In other countries, the trend toward more control of the private sector continues.

Overall, then, the picture in the coming years will undoubtedly become more complex. The black and white differences between the private and state sector we have seen in the past may become muddied as governments regulate the private sector and make efforts to improve the economic performance of the state-owned sector. We may see a greater mix of state and private firms (including more mixed state and private ownership), and wider variations in behavior.

EFFICIENCY AND WELFARE

The effect of government ownership of industry on the economic well-being of Western European nations is hotly debated in European politics,[2] and an impressive array of arguments is marshaled on both sides. Who is right? We have no doubt that the nationalized firm is constrained and oriented by politicization such that its labor markets, other factor markets, capital markets, and product markets depart from market conditions of efficient resource allocation. We do not argue that all political interventions reduce societal welfare; where markets are imperfect and defective, appropriate state intervention may enhance efficiency and improve resource allocation. But is efficiency improved by the public policies toward the state firms? Let us look at two of the most common interventions and assess their impact on a nation's economic welfare.

First take the case of a state-owned electricity (or steel) company that is told to purchase coal from the state-owned company at higher than the market cost. This practice is followed in Great Britain, France, and West Germany, and no doubt elsewhere. Is this policy in the nation's interest? The winners are the coal miners who presumably would have to find other jobs if the state did not insist that they be subsidized. The losers are the consumers of electricity or steel who could have purchased these products more inexpensively if the company had been able to minimize its production costs. If both enterprises operate at a loss, the taxpayers also are losers. If consumers and taxpayers both lose, and the coal workers win, one could argue that there are more losers than winners, and that the policy seems irrational. Yet, as James Q. Wilson points out, when political benefits are concentrated in a relatively small group and the economic costs are diffused throughout the society, a number of policies that prove to be extremely costly to the society at large are tolerated.[3] This is an altogether typical use of the state firm—to benefit one sector of the population while passing on the costs to consumers or taxpayers. In individual cases, the loss in efficiency may not be great, but in the aggregate it is substantial.

Why would nations subsidize their coal industries in this way? Two arguments are given. One, the political argument, is that the coal miners are politically strong and have a great deal at stake in this policy. They are able to politically out-muscle the taxpayers and consumers who presumably are only marginally affected by higher-priced products and heavier losses. The second argument is economic. Nations must preserve their domestic coal industries—even if they are inefficient—to maintain the security of supply in case of a national emergency or interruption in foreign supplies. The wisdom of the policy depends on whether this method of insuring a supply of fuel for times of crisis is cheap or expensive, compared to alternative approaches to the problem. The question of the effect on the "general welfare" would depend on whether the least expensive solution was chosen. Most observers believe government policies which lavishly subsidize domestic coal usage are based more on political than on economic factors.

Consider a second case. Employees in an unprofitable state enterprise demand a raise in pay. The company is a major exporter of manufactured (high value-added) goods such as planes or cars. Should the government give the employees the pay raise or endure a possibly protracted strike? The issue of winners and losers is more complex in this case. If the employees are given the raise, production continues uninterrupted, orders are filled on time, and the nation's balance of payments benefits. The winners are the employees, and perhaps also holders of the nation's currency, which marginally benefits if exports are strong. The losers are the customers and/or taxpayers, who must pay higher prices, or higher taxes—depending on whether the price of the product rises to cover new wages or whether the firm simply incurs more losses because of the higher labor costs. If the raise means increased costs of the exported good, higher prices may create a drop in export demand. Then the government may wind up subsidizing exports to maintain the plant's workforce—a loss to the general society, but a gain for the small group of workers who received the raise.

Is a huge state commitment to a new high technology industry, with the expectation that no profit will be achieved for many years ever in the public interest? Should the nation purchase the product from a foreign supplier, or allow a foreign-owned firm to build, own, and operate the plant instead? Has it been in France's best interest to break even on Renault for many years, thereby keeping Volkswagen and other foreign producers from dominating the French market, or would this money have been better spent elsewhere? Should Britain and Italy subsidize BL and Alfa-Romeo in spite of their heavy losses? Are the Germans and Austrians foolish to run state-owned steel firms at continual losses, or are these losses offset by the political tranquility these exports to the Eastern bloc allegedly buy? At what level of profits or losses is it cheaper for a nation to let a firm go bankrupt? One can do cost-benefit analyses on each of these public policy dilemmas and evaluate the outcomes in terms of social welfare. But "rational" considerations are not decisive. The arguments for and against each are political in character. State ownership (especially in a democracy) means that more and more economic decisions will be made at the governmental level, not the level of the firm. And it is well established that the proliferation of extramarket processes at the expense of market processes becomes a serious drag on efficiency and the general level of economic well-being in a society.

Nationalization continues to be an article of faith for socialists who assume that replacing private ownership with public ownership means that the public interest will be served. A large share of the voting population of Europe—certainly the labor unions and much of academe—continues to hold this belief. For politicians, nationalization is a short-term refuge from pragmatic difficulties. State-controlled companies can, in fact, "solve" certain specific problems. They *can* arrest unemployment, save a failing firm, keep an industry from passing into foreign control, channel investment into selected projects, involve workers in decision making, and follow a wide range of government directives and expectations. Nationalized companies can pursue these specific social policies.

But what is the wisdom of a policy of stressing many goals? One issue is, how many goals can be pursued at once, and are they consistent? The danger is that objectives are blurred, managers do not know what is expected of them, and the firm muddles along. In this familiar case, the nationalized firm's performance will not be subject to objective evaluation at all.

A second issue is the economic wisdom of expecting nationalized firms to pursue social goals. Clearly a point is reached where the social benefits come at a high price and the firms become uncompetitive. If, on the other hand, one believes that nationalized firms should adopt the same policies as private firms, the argument that nationalization serves social goals loses its validity.

Politicians who have a survival instinct can be expected to do what is politically popular, not necessarily what is in the society's best interests. Economic efficiency and consumer welfare are not the criteria that politicians think of first when making decisions. It follows that if decisions on state firms' policies are made largely by politicians, there is more than a little reason to doubt whether state-owned firms in democracies contribute to general economic welfare. Indeed, democracies may be less adept at managing socialist institutions efficiently than are authoritarian regimes. Interest group politics can be very costly to a society if a preponderance of anti-market decisions are reached. State ownership of industry vastly enlarges the number of issues which become overtly political. As Abram Bergson notes, "the radical extension of public ownership must greatly increase opportunities for costly bureaucratic distortions and accommodation to constituency politics."[4] He concludes that democratic politics could be "fully as consequential" in harming efficiency as technical economic difficulties. Democracies that nationalize industries face inherent, possibly intractable, problems of politicization which more authoritarian regimes usually can overlook.

WILL THE UNITED STATES NATIONALIZE BUSINESS?

In few countries do politicians attest so vigorously to the virtues of free enterprise and private property as in the United States. The bailout of Lockheed and the guarantee of loans for Chrysler were billed as actions necessary to bolster free enterprise, not nationalization. When outright nationalization of railroads occurs, euphemisms are found to rationalize and explain it. The "destruction" of the railroads "due to government regulation" necessitates "the maintenance of service necessary for private business and the public," we are told. Outright failures of private companies are seldom admitted by politicians. One result of such rhetoric is that U.S. industry may become increasingly vulnerable to nationalization—either implicitly or explicitly.

In Europe, many justifications for nationalization are advanced. But could nationalization occur in the United States in the absence of a major socialist party or ideology? There is ample evidence that nationalization does occur under different banners. A pragmatic approach to massive government aid and nationalization has been pursued, albeit reluctantly, by conservative governments in Europe in recent years. The nonideological call in the U.S. could be the "economic necessity" to save giant firms and ailing industries. Political opportunism—the need to win votes and secure political careers—could provide the impetus if the economy collapsed.

Given the political pressures to nationalize economically distressed firms and critical defense industries, nationalization could occur, and to some degree already has, in the United States. It does not appear that marginally profitable firms or successful banks, would be nationalized here as they have been in France. Rather, a pattern closer to nationalizations in Britain and Sweden would be more likely in the United States. The arguments about maintaining employment, national sovereignty, and public services could be used to justify government takeovers. In Sweden, a government committed to turning the tide against state control was elected, yet with the adverse turn of world trade the Fälldin government resorted to "saving" (*i.e.*, nationalizing) more companies than the socialist government that preceded it had in thirty years in office. Despite the ideological opposition to nationalization in the United States, a severe depression, or increased competition from foreign firms, could cause economic crisis for U.S. companies and lead to government takeovers. While this scenario may seem unlikely now, the probability is higher than is normally admitted.

Maintaining the vigorous economic health of American industry is the main prescriptión offered to protect it from nationalization. To expect continuous success for every large company is, however, contrary to the tenets of capitalism. Schumpeter has most clearly explained the process of "creative destruction" in capitalism and the need to shift resources to the most dynamic sectors of the economy. If this process is curtailed by public opinion and government intervention, the potential growth of the capitalist system is limited. At the same time, it is unreasonable to expect private firms to compete against heavily subsidized firms—either state-owned or private. Free trade requires that all players use roughly the same rules. American firms have recently been trying to convince their government that the future of many private industries is closely intertwined with the nationalization and subsidization policies of foreign governments.

PRECEDENTS FOR STATE OWNERSHIP

Americans have debated the appropriate role of government in the economy since the founding of the Republic. Alexander Hamilton and Thomas Jefferson, for example, had different philosophies about the place of government in the economy. In the main, the arguments have centered on federal versus state powers, the role of government in regulating the market place, defining property rights, and the distribution of income in the society. Private ownership was assumed in the United States to be the cornerstone of political freedom and economic progress. Democratic capitalism has been the only political-economic system seriously discussed by the two major parties. Advocacy of socialism, state ownership, Marxism, or communism has meant political suicide. Yet at a few points in U.S. history, the state ownership option has been cautiously adopted. An examination of the circumstances that caused the state to invest in business enterprises and the precedents for state ownership in America can provide a number of clues as to the possible directions for future nationalization.

THE TENNESSEE VALLEY AUTHORITY

A notable exception to America's dislike of state ownership was the development of the Tennessee Valley Authority in the 1930s. Franklin D. Roosevelt, despite the mutual distrust between him and the business community, had no strong socialist, or even welfare, ideology. Rather, Roosevelt was the consummate political pragmatist, elected to office in the midst of the nation's longest and deepest depression. His willingness to experiment with the TVA was due largely to concern about the depression in the South and to the unwillingness of private ventures to take on a project with such large costs and high risks. Nonetheless, it was a distinct departure from the government's previous role in the U.S. economy. Vociferous critics to the contrary, the TVA did not herald the beginning of a large socialized sector. Given the possibilities of the times, Roosevelt experimented remarkably little with state ownership. State ownership of liquor stores in the individual states represented a more extensive nationalization than the federal government undertook. But this was caused more by the temperance movement and the desire to raise revenue than by a desire for socialism.

THE RAILROADS

The government's reluctant takeover of the disintegrating and bankrupt passenger railroad systems in the United States provides an example of partial takeover of an industry similar to those in Europe. There, railroads have been owned by the state for decades, but in the United States the step was taken as a last ditch effort in 1971, when Amtrak was formed to maintain passenger service to certain geographic regions. Today most of Amtrak's problems are political. Congress seems to think passenger service can be run profitably, although no other passenger train service in the world is. The result is that the railroad system is starved for funds to maintain its cars and track beds. Great Britain spent $728 million to subsidize its rail passenger system in 1978; Amtrak, a much larger system, received only $500 million. France spent $930 million in the same year; and Japan allocated $4.1 billion to subsidize its rail system. Paradoxically, "The United States is currently contributing $2.4 billion every year to the World Bank to help railroad development in other countries . . ."[1]

Can transportation services be supplied better and less expensively by private companies? Have long-haul trucks, traveling on subsidized highways, been given an unfair competitive edge over railroads? The questions of subsidies and regulations lead directly to a consideration of whether the railroad passenger service system could have been made profitable with appropriate changes in public policy. Many economists blame improper government regulation for the decline of the railroads and their present sorry state.

Regulation, not nationalization, has been the usual American response to monopolies. Our private public utilities contrast with European state owned utilities. When regulation seemed unnecessary and outdated, as a result of new competition in telecommunications for AT&T from IBM and others, the deregulation of the industry was welcomed in nearly all political corners. United States instincts are to return to the principles of private ownership and a free and unregulated market, as opposed to the trend toward nationalization so common elsewhere.

POSSIBLE TARGETS FOR NATIONALIZATION

MILITARY AND DEFENSE FIRMS

In 1969, Lockheed, one of the nation's largest defense companies, overran its budget on a government cargo jet by $2 billion. Company officials informed the Pentagon that they would need $600 million at once to continue work on four other military projects. At the same time, Britain's Rolls-Royce company, supplying the engines for the Lockheed TriStar, ran into a similar financial crisis that led to nationalization by the government. Lockheed found that the banks would not loan it additional money without a government guarantee. This was finally approved, amid much controversy, by a one-vote margin in the U.S. Senate in 1971. The government agreed to guarantee up to $250 million in loans to keep Lockheed alive.

The rationale for the loan was national defense. Boeing, however, cut back its labor force to under 40 percent of previous levels when it ran into similar trouble. Cynics pointed out that Lockheed was located in a state with many more votes (and Congressmen) than Boeing. It pays a firm in trouble, it was said, to be located in a state crucial to the reelection of a president.

From the perspective of ten years, the lessons of the Lockheed experience are not totally clear. Lockheed is still in business, although at a reduced level. Its future looks less bright in the commercial market where it seems to be having increased problems competing with Boeing and Airbus Industrie. Boeing is perhaps a much stronger company than Lockheed ten years later, possibly because of its enforced belt tightening. Boeing is one of the most efficient industrial companies in the country, even though the highly subsidized Airbus Industrie is steadily increasing its world market share at Boeing's expense. Could Lockheed also have survived by cutting back and laying off 70,000 employees? The answer is unclear. In retrospect it appears that the Lockheed "solution" had far less short-range impact on the community—and probably on the politicians as well.

Loan guarantees seem more successful than outright nationalization if a nation wishes to avoid continuing subsidies to industry. Yet to use public funds to bolster unprofitable firms contradicts traditional economic, though not necessarily political, wisdom. Given the new complications of international competition (especially foreign subsidies, nontariff barriers, and nationalized firms), the economic point of view becomes clouded. As a result, public policy toward domestic firms in financial difficulty becomes more perplexing. Each case is examined separately and settled largely on political grounds.

What does this imply for the future of private business? Is further government intervention and involvement likely? Is nationalzation a possibility, high probability, or inevitable? It is at least worth noting that outside the United States military and defense industries are nearly always state-owned.[1]

BASKET CASES

Chrysler In 1980, the Chrysler Corporation obtained a government loan guarantee for $1.5 billion, following the precedent set by Lockheed a decade earlier. In the case of Chrysler, however, national defense was not the main argument. The Defense Department had insisted that Chrysler's defense projects be spun off into a separate corporation to prevent interruptions in delivery in case the company did go bankrupt. Obviously, the Defense Department had some concern over Chrysler's future viability.

But the basic argument in Chrysler's case was the need to maintain employment in regions where the unemployment rate was already high. Company employment fell from a 1979 figure of 141,000 to 79,000 by December 1980. Almost all of this employment was in large urban states with the accompanying political clout that a large employer can generate. Indeed, without this employment distribution it is doubtful the Carter administration would have pushed the $1.5 billion Chrysler loan guarantee through Congress.

The employment argument was bolstered by two additional arguments; first, that Chrysler had faced unfair foreign competition; and second, that government regulation mandating fuel efficiency, safety and antipollution devices had increased Chrysler's costs. Such costs, it was argued, affected Chrysler more than General Motors or Ford because it sold fewer cars. Thus its unit costs were higher, making the company uncompetitive against General Motors.

Chrysler's future at this time is brighter, but still uncertain. High interest rates slowed sales of automobiles in the United States and increased Chrysler's costs as well. Whether Chrysler can raise the capital to develop enough new models to compete profitably with both foreign auto manufacturers and General Motors is a major question.

Indeed, the future of the Ford Motor Company in the U.S. is in doubt. In the last several years, only its overseas divisions have been profitable. Ford also must develop a whole new line of cars, but lacks the capital to do so rapidly. It is not clear that its profitable (protected) overseas operations can keep the company afloat forever. Otherwise, Ford might either become a shadow of itself or an overseas auto manufacturer operating mainly in markets protected from Japanese competition, as is now typical of most of the world auto market.

U.S. Steel U.S. Steel is the nation's largest and, by many accounts, most inefficient steelmaker. Company officials have long argued that Japanese and European steelmakers, many of them state-owned, have been "dumping" their steel in the American market to the detriment of U.S. Steel and the other domestic steel companies. Indeed, in 1977 the Carter administration instituted a "trigger-price" mechanism to keep out cheaper foreign steel.

A study by Merrill Lynch, however, has shown that since 1959 most of the gains made by foreign steelmakers in the U.S. market have been at the expense of U.S. Steel. This is not surprising. Since J. P. Morgan put U.S. Steel together from a number of different steel firms in 1901, U.S. Steel has had a reputation as a laggard and inefficient company.

Dwight MacDonald commented in his memoirs on his reactions to U.S. Steel after completing an extensive series of articles in *Fortune* in the 1930s. "The more research I gathered, the more it became evident that the biggest steel company in the world benefited neither its workers (wages were then low). . . . its customers (prices were kept high). . . . nor its owners (who got slim dividends)."[2] The main thing that has changed since then is that the workers are now among the highest paid in any industry, and certainly the highest paid steelworkers in the world. On top of that, U.S. Steel's plants are truly antiquated by world standards.

It is not surprising that U.S. Steel is so vulnerable to more efficient steelmakers abroad. The success of steel exports from European state-owned firms into the United States is more surprising—until one remembers the gargantuan subsidies European state-owned firms enjoy. Their policies are little more than the export of unemployment to nations willing to buy their steel.

Nonetheless, U.S. Steel is a weak reed upon which to base a case for steel tariffs. Its decrepit state is more a result of self-inflicted wounds and inept management than of damage caused by subsidized European competitors. In the long run, the hopes for the domestic steel industry lie in major modernization, wage reductions, and capital improvement programs. Government policy should recognize the necessity of having a modern and efficient steel industry—for reasons of national defense, if none other. Duties should be levied only against state-owned and state-subsidized imports—and only on the condition that domestic modernization take place. If inefficient steel companies are protected from foreign competitors without modernization, the industry will remain a museum piece as profits go to diversification. The eventual pressures for nationalization in the name of national defense would become irresistible, which would only make things worse.

HIGH TECHNOLOGY

Semiconductors *The New York Times* reported in mid-1981 that, "As the Government ponders legislation designed to revitalize American industry, it is being hit with demands from a somewhat unexpected sector—the U.S. semiconductor industry." Spokesmen for the semiconductor industry, one of the most innovative, prosperous, and rapidly growing industries in the United States, claim to be suffering from the same problem vexing steel and autos— intense and subsidized foreign competition. This competition comes particularly from Japan. But even the conservative British government is assisting a state industry in this field, as is socialist France. The potential competition will become even more serious as other foreign governments become involved.

U.S. microchip manufacturers say it is hard for them to raise the money they need for the new equipment required by rapidly changing technology. But banks have been worried that competition will force the semi-conductor industry into severe economic straits, as the automobile and steel industries have been, and they are reluctant to risk their money. They also see other nations setting up and supporting their own semi-conductor industries, thus curtailing the potential market for exports. American firms argue that they could eventually be driven out of the industry they originated unless they can raise the capital to keep up.

Government aid, particularly in the form of incentives for research and development, is being solicited by the industry. It argues that it should be supported because it is competing against subsidized foreign firms, because its products are crucial to the national defense, and because it is an infant industry. The fact that even Margaret Thatcher is willing to invest her government's money in developing this new industry in Great Britain suggests its national strategic importance. Foreign competition from Japan and European state-owned firms could precipitate a crisis for the U.S. semiconductor industry. The military might demand that the government act to protect its future source of the chips necessary for almost all advanced weapons. Thus, even in the United States, state-sponsored or state-owned firms may be forthcoming in order to assure that investment in industry will occur.

Aerospace The Airbus, Europe's answer to American world airliner dominance, has been supported by the political/economic resources of six European governments in research, development, testing, and production. A document published by the French National Assembly in December 1979 which said in part: "In this economic world war, it is vital to break the quasimonopoly that American manufacturers have for medium and long ranged commercial aircraft," and the French have responded accordingly.

To help Boeing and other American firms export in the face of this type of competition, the U.S. Export-Import Bank was created. For the first time since World War II, however, the bank showed a loss. The European governments have encouraged sales of the Airbus by offering especially low interest rates and favorable terms. U.S. firms cannot get commercial bank financing to sell airlines to emerging nations. Thus without the Eximbank, the $35 billion in sales over the past ten years would have been impossible, and the nation's trade balance would have been seriously harmed.

Another argument for U.S. government support of the Eximbank is national defense. Engineering technology developed for commercial applications has been incorporated into the production of military equipment. Commercial activity maintains a large pool of highly skilled engineers and craftsmen who can be made available to military programs in case of national emergencies.

Thus, the government-subsidized competition represents a major threat to one of the United States' strongest industries. Much as a conservative laissez-faire government may favor free trade, even Adam Smith recognized the importance of national defense as an argument. Further, employment concerns create strong pressures to aid domestic firms threatened by foreign state-owned firms. It is questionable whether an American government, regardless of ideology, could avoid supporting a failing major industry with national defense capability. In the long run, the escalating capital costs of creating and producing new airplanes make it more and more unlikely that the financial markets will be able to handle the job. This is another force that could lead to eventual government control, and even ownership of this industry.

THE PUBLIC POLICY ALTERNATIVES

Over the next two decades the United States is likely to face a continuing decline in the competitive position of its industry. The danger signals can be seen in recent developments in a number of once-dominant U.S. industries:

1. The steel industry already has its share of troubles, but new production from state-owned companies in Brazil and South Korea (often financed, ironically, by long-term loans from U.S. banks) will provide even stiffer competition over the next two decades.

2. The future of the U.S. auto industry, having shrunk its capacity at the same time that the Japanese industry has vigorously grown, is doubtful. The Japanese protected their home market while building up their auto industry, and the European countries provided aid and protection to their industry. The future of both Ford and Chrysler is problematic, and even General Motors looks less powerful than it did a few years ago.

3. In consumer electronics, where it used to be the world leader, the United States has essentially thrown in the towel. For example, there are no U.S. producers of videotape recorders.

4. In the microprocessor and semiconductor industry, the United States has a clear lead in technology, research, and development. But with government-financed investment, the Japanese, who are more efficient in production, have quickly captured up to one-half of the U.S. market. The Europeans strive to keep the United States and Japan out of their microprocessor markets while their governments underwrite new investment. Although the United States developed the microprocessor industry, it is unlikely to become a major exporter and, indeed, is even unable to preserve the domestic market for its own firms.

5. In computers, the battle is just shaping up between American and Japanese firms. Although U.S. companies have had success in marketing computers in Europe and Japan, these are usually not exports, but sales of computers manufactured in those nations.

6. In aerospace, the prognosis for U.S. industry is more pessimistic today than at any time since World War II. For the first time in twenty years, the Europeans have mounted a stunningly successful campaign to capture a large share of the market for jet aircraft. Boeing is now dominant only in the U.S. market, while Airbus is dominant in sales outside the U.S. A new factor in the competitive equation is the Japanese interest in aerospace; the Japanese government has targeted this industry for major financial help. The early development of Japan's aerospace industry is impressive, according to close observers of new Japanese areospace plant and equipment.

7. In the photocopying industry, the United States is dominant, but a number of energetic Japanese companies are increasing their market share.

8. In data communications and telecommunications equipment, American firms lead in technology, but their inability to sell to state-owned telecommunications authorities in other countries has destined them to compete mainly in third world markets and in the United States, which are markets open to foreign firms with free access to liberal export funding.

9. In a number of other industries, the United States has experienced a major relative decline—cameras, watches, pianos, motorcycles, machine tools, general machinery, capital goods, construction, and even banking.

The causes and consequences of this relative decline are complex. Studies that attribute the decline in the growth of productivity or to long-run economic forces of comparative advantage (labor costs and other costs of production), management negligence and incompetence, regulation, and other trends have provided important diagnoses of the problem. There is no question that costs must be reduced if U.S. industry is to compete successfully. Yet issues of public policy must also be examined. More than secular economic forces account for the ebb and flow of international trade and the rise and fall of various industries in each nation. Anyone who studies the industrial economies of Japan and Western Europe recognizes that trade policy, industrial policy, and tax policy are variables which affect industrial change, investment, and productivity. Serious analysis of declining, and potentially threatened, industries in the United States must acknowledge these government policies as partial determinants of economic trends.

The United States has led the free world in developing a trade policy based on the premise that other nations could be persuaded to adopt policies that resemble its own. The evidence now suggests that these nations, perhaps understandably, have not consistently cooperated in this endeavor. The trend toward nationalization and subsidization of industry and invention of ingenious nontariff barriers are making a mockery of the basic tenets of the international free trading system.

What policy alternatives exist? First, the United States can toughen its enforcement of trade laws that are now self-consciously enforced or completely ignored. When other nations subsidize their industries, the United States should not hesitate to invoke countervailing duties and adopt other statutory remedies. This is not protectionism; it is the enforcement of mutually agreed procedures which govern international trade. United States enforcement of these laws would be met by vigorous protests from the international community, but these protests should not distress the United States. Finger-pointing at U.S. protectionism is a time-honored European and Japanese ploy when their own policies are even more protectionistic.

The United States could also begin to monitor much more closely violations of subsidization codes and dumping laws by foreign industries. It has become routine for the Japanese to sell products more cheaply in the United States than in Japan—a fact that U.S. tourists in Japan have long known. Prosecuting subsidization and dumping requires the government willingness to prosecute, and the availability of sufficient staff. At a minimum, a special staff to monitor the trade and subsidization policies of each major industry would be necessary.

Another approach would be to make further efforts to change the behavior of other nations, as the United States has done in the past. The United States could attempt to write new laws and sign new treaties that insist subsidization of industry be stopped. *But the ability of the United States to persuade, or coerce, other nations to live by the rules that govern American capitalism is rapidly diminishing, if it ever existed.* The United States has been capable of getting major trading partners to agree on principles of trade, but not on policies to implement the principles. Its mistake has been thinking that other countries could be convinced to be like it.

The difficulty of effectively policing protectionist practices should not be understated. Protection may be direct and overt, as with tariffs and quotas, and fewer difficulties of detection and proof are encountered. Covert forms of protection include Japanese "administrative guidance" to potential domestic customers and discriminatory administration of safety, health, and environmental regulations against competitive foreign products. Such practices are gaining in frequency and importance around the world, especially in the nationalized industries, and they are next to impossible to ferret out and subject to the rule of law. Although we strongly support the basic goal of separating trade from politics, we are not optimistic about the chances of success.

The United States could also adopt an explicit export policy. Other nations have an array of specific policies to aid exporting industries, including government services, special financing of long-term contracts, and tax policies that encourage exporting. U.S. policies which encourage exports are timid by comparison, as the controversy over Eximbank financing shows.

The United States needs a set of incentives to those industries which it is in the national interest to retain. Support of supply side economics to strengthen the capital markets is necessary, but specific policies must be designed for particular industries which need to be preserved and modernized. The United States is the only nation in the world, capitalist or socialist, which does not consider whether it should have an auto industry, a computer industry, a steel industry, or an aerospace industry. A coterie of economists has persuaded generations of students and business executives that capital markets left to their own devices will solve all problems with perfect efficiency, and everyone will be better off as a result. This model assumes that companies compete with no subsidies or government-conferred advantages, and the model no longer exists in the real world—if indeed it ever did.

The United States is still lagging on tax policies that encourage saving and investment. The traditional remedies of creating investment incentives through tax and depreciation policies retain their importance. Yet it is unclear that substantial incentives have been created by the Reagan tax policy changes, which do little more than roll back recent bracket creep. The Reagan administration's experiment in supply side economics may increase savings and offer new incentives to American capitalism, but will the incentives be sufficient to "reindustrialize" America, and will the policies operate quickly enough to make competitors and champions out of industries now at some state of arteriosclerosis? There is the further question of where any new savings will be invested. If savings go into real estate, precious metals, collectibles, or foreign investment, they will not improve the productivity of industry. Thus tax policies, such as eliminating double taxation, are at best a partial solution. They may not steer investment into the industries that need modernization.

A further area for reform is a change in antitrust laws which now place U.S. firms on an unequal footing with foreign competitors. For example, outside the United States, export cartels are normally permitted. The justification given is that firms can reduce overhead costs of exports and counter the market power of foreign buying cartels. Foreign exporters collude on price, quality, quantity, design, and marketing arrangements, and a wide range of cartels exists worldwide for many products. Japan uses recession cartels put together by MITI to help struggling industries get through difficult spots in the business cycle, as do the Europeans. As Ezra Vogel has said, "We cannot continue to rely on antitrust laws to determine our nation's industrial policy."[3]

In matters of industrial policy and trade policy, the United States should notice what the Europeans and Japanese do, not what they say. Our major trading partners follow their national interests over formal compliance with laws and treaties, and they are not bashful about it. They defend their markets through price agreements, market cartels, subsidies, trade regulations, quotas, and import controls. These policies fly in the face of the recommendations of welfare economists and are in disregard of trade laws and treaties. The U.S. must either accept these policies for what they are and formulate our own policies in that light, or continue to be a nation increasingly committed to unilateral free trade.

In the next two decades the U.S. economy will be more exposed to the forces of international competition than at ony other time in the twentieth century. Other nations have outperformed the U.S. economy in growth rates for over twenty years now, and although the U.S. economy remains the largest in the world, it will no longer be if recent trends continue. A public policy to stop the relative decline of U.S. industry and restore investment and productivity growth is sorely needed.

The European experience suggests that nationalization to save "sunset" industries, or promote "sunrise" industries, is disappointing and costly. Nationalization to save declining industries entails enormous and unnecessary costs. Reorganization and redeployment of resources becomes a cumbersome and drawn-out process. In France, the elite meritocracy of planning officials, may be able to get things done expeditiously and with a minimum of obstruction. But Britain's experience with declining state-owned industries suggests that decisions become thoroughly politicized. A political tradition of due process requires that decisions can be challenged and rechallenged prior to implementation. U.S. legal and political traditions are more British than French; hence, substantial government ownership in the United States would stalemate many decisions in the economy. Even more than in Europe, the management of an American state-owned company would be likely to find itself challenged by politicians and citizens on every decision. It would endlessly be in court to defend and enforce its policies.

Nationalized Companies

The most successful advanced capitalist European nation in recent years, West Germany, has been the most reluctant to expand the role of its state-owned firms as has Switzerland as well. Japan also follows this pattern. To be sure, state-owned companies exist in Japan and West Germany: Lufthansa and Japan Air Lines, the telephone systems, Japan's tobacco monopoly, and Germany's steel, aluminum, oil, and (some) automotive interests. These are important contrasts with the American economy. Yet what is most notable about the German and Japanese cases is their reliance on other tools of industrial promotion, aside from nationalization. Research and development aid, public purchasing preferences, credit allocation, grants in aid to high technology industries, remodernization assistance to inefficient industries, and covert protectionism in selected sectors—these are the hallmarks of West German and Japanese industrial policy. Indeed, the success of Germany and Japan may largely lie in the fact that they have not resorted to nationalization to solve their problems nearly as much as Great Britain, France, Italy, Canada, or the Scandinavian countries. The major "locomotive" and high technology industries responsible for the development of the West German and Japanese economies have been those in the private sector. West Germany and Japan have followed industrial and trade policies which built up and strengthened the international competitive power of the private sector—and this is a lesson that the United States should remember.

NATIONALIZATION
AND THE FUTURE
OF CAPITALISM

Industry in Europe and in some other areas of the world appears to be in the midst of a transformation from private to state ownership. During the 1970s, governments not only functioned as regulators and tax collectors but emerged as entrepreneurs on an increasingly international scale. One explanation for this is the success of socialist ideology in many democratic elections. The other cause of the new nationalization is the desire to assert national control over economies by guaranteeing a national presence in key industries. Nations accomplish this in two ways: First, by "defensively" rescuing firms in financial trouble (due to out-of-control costs or overcapacity); and, second, by "offensively" investing state funds in the rapid expansion and diversification of sectors where private capital is hesitant to invest.

Multinational business is clearly no longer the exclusive preserve of private capitalists. Among the fifty largest non-U.S. companies in 1982, twenty firms had significant proportions of state participation in ownership. The French and Italian firms in that group were either owned outright (as with ENI or Renault where 95 percent state ownership is shared with 5 percent employee shareholding) or the state had strong minority holdings. State ownership has also gained ground in Great Britain and in the third world (*e.g.,* Iran and Brazil). Almost every major company that has emerged in the third world in the past few years has been state-owned. The largest industrial companies in France, Mexico, Austria, Argentina, Brazil, and India are government-owned.

The extent of the transformation of European industry toward state ownership can be seen in a brief summary of the industries most affected by the new nationalization.

149

Nationalized Companies

Automobiles Today the European automobile industry is half nationalized, the major state firms being Renault, BL Ltd., Alfa Romeo, Volvo Car, and SEAT—not to mention the state's important stakes in Volkswagen and BMW. The spread in state ownership in automobiles has dramatically changed the nature and competitive strategy of the European industry in the past decade.

Electronics and Computers All European nations have a national plan (either formal or de facto) for the electronics and computer industries. State ownership is not the only element in such plans, but it is often a major one—as in Britain, France, and Italy.

Aerospace All of the U.S.'s competition in civil and military aviation is government-owned and government-controlled. Airbus Industrie, a consortium of state-owned and state-controlled firms, has captured most of the new sales outside the United States. European governments have given unequivocal assurance to customers that they stand financially behind their companies.

Oil The world oil industry was transformed in the 1970s with the appearance of state oil companies, while the assets of many big multinational oil companies were nationalized. State-owned oil companies now produce over 85 percent of the noncommunist world's oil, and crude oil buyers now have to look to the national oil company and accept its terms to obtain future supplies. State oil companies are already diversifying downstream, and if these trends continue, the future of the private oil industry is uncertain.

Steel Most European steel is now made in state-owned firms, and six of the top fourteen European steel manufacturers are government-owned companies—British Steel, Finsider, Usinor, Salzgitter, Cockerill, and Sacilor. Only Germany maintains a large private steel industry.

Airlines A privately owned international airline is an anamoly in Western Europe, as elsewhere in the world outside the United States. With the exception of Switzerland, all the European nations have state-owned flag carriers, and in the past ten years the state-owned airlines have increased their share of international passenger traffic from under 70 percent to over 85 percent. While Pan Am and TWA have suffered big cuts in fleets and employment, Air France, KLM, Lufthansa, and Japan Air Lines have increased employment and market share.

Pulp and Paper The European forest products industry, particularly pulp and paper, is centered in Scandinavia, where the state has taken over a number of companies in the past decade and is now the major owner in the entire sector. A series of state takeovers and subsidies has kept the industry alive, despite lower-cost producers in the United States and Canada.

Mining All types of mining—coal and metals—have increasingly come under state ownership in Europe and the third world nations. Today state companies control over a third of noncommunist production of iron ore—the major state producers being Brazil, Liberia, Sweden, and Venezuela. Mining of nonferrous metals has followed the same pattern. Ten years ago all copper production was in private hands. Now governments control well over 60 percent of the non-OECD world's copper mining, smelting, and refining output, and their share is growing. Coal mining is almost entirely a state enterprise in Europe.

Aluminum The aluminum industry came under increasing state ownership in Europe in the past decade. Germany and Austria's state aluminum companies increased production, while Norway and France vigorously expanded their state-owned aluminum sector. Austrian and Norwegian state-owned aluminum companies are diversifying from primary aluminum into manufactured aluminum products.

Telecommunications Services The market for telecommunications transmissions is made principally of state-owned PTT's (post office, telephone and telegraph). None of the telecommunications markets of the industrialized countries outside the United States is open to true international competition, since the PTT monopolies in Europe want to slow down technological development and preserve the market for themselves.

Office Equipment European governments have used state firms to keep foreign competition from taking over the burgeoning office equipment industry. Thus, Britain's National Enterprise Board invested 50 million in Nexos, its office automation subsidiary, and Germany used the 44 percent state-owned Volkswagen to take over TriumphAdler, the office equipment manufacturer.

Others In shipbuilding, biotechnology, broadcasting, engineering, construction, banking, and insurance, the state share grows from year to year.

From its beginning in the public utilities, state ownership has expanded vigorously into the extractive industries, manufacturing, and service industries (shipping, airlines, tourism, and hotels). Aside from automobiles, the only area where state companies remain relatively insignificant is the consumer goods sector. Thus, in the past decade or two, the European economy (and many third world economies) has changed from a structure where government ownership outside of the public utilities was unusual to the new situation where it is difficult to find a sector where states do not have an important stake.

Nationalization is not likely to be reversed in Europe, even with the election of right-of-center governments from time to time. Political arguments that make nationalization attractive to voters, coupled with the broad base of state companies eager to expand, acquire, and diversify, make any roll-back of nationalization unlikely. As William Shepherd concludes, "A further rise of public enterprise in coming decades . . . is likely to dilute further the dominance of the private corporation."[1]

THE DECLINE OF EUROPE

Nationalization seems to be symptomatic of a broader economic malaise and economic decline in Western Europe. European power is infinitesimal compared to the preeminent position it enjoyed at the beginning of the twentieth century. In part, this relative decline was caused by the success of American capitalism, but more recently the economies of Western Europe have found it increasingly easy to drift toward nationalization and socialism. As Paul Seabury of the University of California at Berkeley has stated, it is almost incomprehensible to anyone who takes a long view of twentieth-century history that today's Europeans are the same people whose empires not long ago governed the destinies of large parts of the world.[2] There are serious doubts that European industry will be able to break the grip of the socialist unions and socialist parties. What were once private economic decisions in Europe have become political decisions. Indeed, political debates in Europe are virtually about no issues except how to make and slice the economic pie.

Grounds for pessimism can be found in almost every European nation. France has socialism in name as well as in fact. Indeed, many observers of French politics believe that France is lost to private enterprise for many years, perhaps indefinitely. Sweden, prior to 1973, made a clear separation between the private sector and the welfare state—in fact, a prosperous private sector was once regarded by many left-of-center politicans and academicians as a necessary condition for the welfare state. Now the intervention of the government in industry's ownership structure has become more direct and extensive, with predictable effects on performance. Leftists are playing a bigger role in the Netherlands. Socialist governments control France, Sweden, and Spain. In Belgium and Ireland, almost every major industry is either heavily subsidized, or state-owned, and crippling work rules imperil structural change. Great Britain will see a new government some day, and the Marxist infiltration of the left wing of the Labour party has been far-reaching. Even Prime Minister Thatcher has been able to do little to roll back the government budget and the nationalized sector of the economy. West Germany, still the bulwark of European capitalism, has moved rapidly in the direction of the welfare state, with government expenditures now as high as 50 percent of GNP.

If these trends in Western Europe continue—and they seem likely to—the United States will eventually be forced to reevaluate its foreign policy and U.S. industry to evaluate its investment and expansion policies. Private capitalists in Europe have already calculated the risks inherent in recent political trends there and have shifted their money elsewhere insofar as possible. A shift away from the basic values of private ownership of business has taken place in Europe and has already undermined the structure of capitalism there. The international economic goal of the United States—to encourage other nations to adopt private enterprise—has failed in Europe.

The future interests of the United States would appear to lie with the most dynamic, growing, productive, energetic new capitalist success stories in the world today, the nations on the Pacific rim—Japan, South Korea, Singapore, Malaysia, Taiwan, and Australia. Industrial civilization is clearly shifting to these economies, and they may soon achieve competitive productive parity with the United States, leaving Europe far behind.

Even if Europe's future is not quite as bleak as we fear, the United States will need to build new trade relationships in the next decade because of the profound ideological changes that have occurred in the European economies. Nationalization and pervasive state ownership are simply not compatible with the concepts of free market economics and free international trade. The structure of these new trade relationships will be up to the United States as much as to the Europeans, but the major problem in developing new international economic agreements is likely to be the reluctance of the European nations to surrender autonomy in national economic policy making. The extension of nationalization in European industry raises the possibility that the United States may increasingly set international trading policy on a bilateral basis with Japan, ignoring Europe. Despite Japan's significant protectionist proclivities—which must be faced head on—they appear to be less significant than Europe's isolationist combination of growing nationalization and protectionism.

ALTERNATIVE SCENARIOS FOR AMERICAN CAPITALISM

What will these developments portend for the future of American capitalism? All we can do is suggest a number of alternatives for the future that now appear possible. We will attempt to spell out what we see as the major alternatives and their apparent consequences.

MARKET CAPITALISM: SCENARIO 1

This version of the future might best be called "roll back the clock," or return to a world where the economic role of government is severely constrained. How much can a government—even one as conservative as the Reagan administration—roll back the clock to an era not seen in the United States since before the 1930s? The likely answer is: not a great deal.

The Reagan administration was able to do both more and less than people expected. Certainly Reaganomics achieved more than the Republican administrations of Presidents Nixon and Ford in turning to market forces and decentralized decision making for the American economy. However, despite the original political rhetoric about the new federalism and getting government off the back of business, the main achievement of Reagan's administration was to change the budget priorities rather than change regulations. Pollution, safety, consumer, and various other regulations were not repealed, as many of Reagan's early business supporters had expected. While the Reagan administration cut back severely on most social, educational, and welfare expenditures, it did not change the laws that had been passed during the previous fifty years to create a capitalist welfare state, regulated by lawyers. Only enforcement policy was modified.

While it was a great pragmatic achievement of the early days of the Reagan administration to cut back tax levels, even liberal economists acknowledge that the stimulating effect that supply-side economists hoped for would have required more drastic tax cuts than were eventually passed by Congress. Both Rostowian and Marxist economists (who viewed the world from opposite poles) believed that long-run business cycles prevented Reagan from restoring full employment and low rates of inflation until the 1990s. They argued that the 1980s were the bottom of a business cycle over which governments had little control. Despite a world-wide depression, however, Reagan did make progress toward reducing the role of the federal government in the American economy and bringing it closer to a form of market capitalism.

A market economy which practices unilateral free trade—as the United States tends to—risks the decline of many industries due to competition from foreign state-owned and state-subsidized firms as well as more efficient and lower-cost capitalist economies, both of which can undersell U.S. firms. Urged on by economists of both political parties, as well as by members of the Reagan administration, the United States may pursue unilateral free trade to the detriment of American business and workers.

A market economy need not eschew tariffs and protection as the history of capitalism teaches. Free trade and market economics may be one intellectual bundle, but they do not have to be one package for public policy, as the most recently successfully growing economies of the world—Japanese and Eastern Asian high-growth economies—demonstrate. Trade policy, then, should be thought of as an integral part of a nation's economic policy. Even if the goal is to lower trade barriers among all trading nations, market capitalism does not require unilateral free trade.

Nationalization, too, is possible under a market economy. Given crisis, high rates of unemployment, and concern about winning elections, even as conservative an administration as Ronald Reagan's could be forced to rescue large firms, however distasteful it might be. Conservative governments have reluctantly nationalized firms in Sweden and Great Britain. Yet other alternatives would have to be exhausted before a U.S. administration resorted to nationalization, and some other name to describe it would have to be found.

The United States is likely to have a more market-oriented economy than any other major industrialized nation in the world for the foreseeable future. It is increasingly possible, however, that the market will operate in some sectors, regulation in others, and full government control, and perhaps state ownership in still other sectors. Such an economy might not be called a pure market economy; but it would be a semimarket economy. Whether it could be called a market capitalist system would depend on how large a segment of the economy made economic decisions outside the market mechanism.

REGULATED CAPITALISM: SCENARIO 2

For the past fifty years in the United States, bursts of regulation increasing government intervention in the economy have been followed by periods of quiescence, followed by another burst of regulation. If we projected the scenario of more of the same for the next twenty years, what would the economy look like by the twenty-first century? The stress of the wars, shortages, inflation, unemployment, and recessions that will be likely to occur will probably increase government's role in decision making in the economy—as it has during the past fifty years. Corporate managers will make decisions within increasingly narrow parameters. A continuing high level of regulatory legislation will mean that government approval will be required for many more business decisions by the end of the century. Business decisions regarding prices, wages, rent, energy control, and so on, if not mandated outright will be sufficiently constrained that profit returns will be lower than we have been used to in the first two-thirds of this century. Therefore, capital shortages will be common among businesses, and this in turn would create more dependence upon government and, indeed, more intervention of government in the economy. Business, however, will be considerably more "responsible" because of laws, regulations, guidelines, and public expectations. In this scenario, a new form of "regulated," or "bureaucratic capitalism," evolves by the turn of the century without any drastic changes in the society—merely by continuing the trends of the past fifty years.

For the average individual, security and regulations will be at even higher levels in the society, but incentives and opportunities to become Edisons, Fords, or Lands will be increasingly slim. Further, discretionary income for most individuals will probably decline as government tax brackets increase to pay for the government's increased role in the society at federal, state, and local levels. Lawyers—including reformers like Nader and regulators in the government bureaucracy, as well as the lawyers in the large corporations and law firms and the judges—would increasingly control the society.

Increasing regulation may be a more realistic scenario than we would prefer. Despite Reagan's protestations and, indeed, those of previous antigovernment politicians such as Carter, little deregulation has, in fact, occurred. Certain fields such as airlines have been deregulated, but no legislation has been passed overall that would roll back the major regulations on business and society that have occurred during the past fifty years.

In such a scenario, the economy would probably become increasingly protectionist, and trade policy more regulated. The idea that the economy and unemployment could be controlled by a protectionistic trade policy follows from the philosophy that government can regulate and make things better. What of nationalization? As unemployment and the balance of trade pose more problems, and as various industries face the crisis of bankruptcy, the pressures for nationalization will mount. The immediate crisis of a particular industry or firm, if large enough, could result in state takeovers either by a conservative or an interventionist administration. Such takeovers might be thought of as only temporary, but experience in Europe suggests that nationalization of this kind is seldom reversed. Regulated capitalism, when extended far enough and long enough, becomes the extinction of capitalism.

PLANNED CAPITALISM: SCENARIO 3

In this scenario national economic planning and a vigorous industrial policy are pursued to solve the critical problems of growth, unemployment, shortages of natural resources, and high rates of inflation. This development could have two causes. These might be first, increasing reliance on government aid and regulation as the economy becomes more crises-ridden or, second a sudden outbreak of war, an international crisis involving natural resources (such as oil), or a prolonged recession or depression. This scenario assumes that our political system remains unchanged, but that regulation eventually increases to include outright planning of the economy in terms of growth, regional development, employment, inflation, wages, rents, and profit margins.

These examples have prototypes in Western Europe in the postwar period. The United States itself, even under conservative governments, has adopted wage and price controls in efforts to meet "planned inflationary rates." A Labour government in Great Britain, in the absence of crisis, requested "permanent wage, price, and profit controls." France's successful economic growth after World War II was attributed by some economists to their planning system, and, indeed, in 1981 a socialist government in France was elected on the political platform of nationalizing the key industries of the economy in order to have greater control and more effective economic planning of the economy. The trend in Europe has been toward more and more planning, in name or in fact, carried out by the government bureaucracy.

Whether planned capitalism, which we assume would also be highly regulated, would adopt such common European forms as state-owned "nationalized" firms is difficult to predict. A possible scenario is that economic problems of energy, inflation, scarce natural resources, unemployment, regional development, and bankruptcy might force the government to take over individual firms (Lockheed, Chrysler, and the railroads serve as precedents). The airlines might also be taken over, as they have been in most foreign nations. These changes could be initiated by public demand for continuation of services (effective transportation), government need for military security (affecting the merchant marine or defense companies), or a dramatic decrease in public trust and confidence in certain businesses (such as banks or the oil industry). A confluence of circumstances and the "right" mix of politicians could change the system to a form of mixed socialism. This could be accomplished by a reluctant Congress, or President, who could suggest no other alternative in time of crisis.

While there is a strong antinationalization bias in the United States, circumstances could create more government firms. We expect some, but not rampant, nationalization to occur in the United States during the remainder of this century.

A variation of this scenario for the future of business is direct partnership between business and government—as in the case of Comsat, the communications satellite developed by American Telephone and Telegraph and the government. In Europe and elsewhere, governments own partial stock in many private firms. In Great Britain, the National Enterprise Board has been given funds to buy stock in firms which need capital for expansion, or might go bankrupt without help. Sweden and Norway have pioneered attempts to aid business in need and, at the same time, to gain government representation on more corporate boards. A partnership between business and government, particularly in new ventures, would be more ideologically acceptable in this country than outright government ownership. Other new ideas—compatible with U.S. ideology—will undoubtedly appear and be advocated during the next few years.

While there has been a strong tradition of opposition to government planning in the United States, in recent years a growing number of important businessmen like Henry Ford II, Irwin Miller, and Michael Blumenthal have come out in favor of some form of national planning. The so called Humphrey-Hawkins and Humphrey-Javits bills have presented the planning issue to Congress. It would be foolhardy to forecast the rest of this century without seriously considering the possibility of some sort of planning mechanism as part of our system of government. An industrial policy to promote sunrise industries and to aid in eliminating the sunset industries (and in transferring their workers to new lines of work) is frequently suggested as unemployment rates mount. Felix Rohatyn and many of the neo-liberals in Congress, as well as economists like Lester Thurow, have urged economic planning in the form of industrial policy as the only solution to the industrial transformation now plaguing advanced industrial countries. An industrial policy would be high on the agenda of a Democratic administration and might well become a solution for certain Republican administrations as an approach to competition with Japan and the new capitalist nations of East Asia as well as the state-owned firms of Europe and the developing nations.

The effect on business of an industrial policy that included economic planning, if carried out on a cooperative basis as is typical of Japan or of presocialist France, might be beneficial. The Japanese and East Asian governments are run essentially by and for the business community, but this degree of corporate power might not be tolerated in the United States. Probusiness planning could reduce uncertainty in the environment and make it possible for firms to plan and invest more rationally on a large scale. The real question would be whether the relationship between planners and business would develop along cooperative or adversary lines. There is reason to doubt that the government, or any group of planners or economists, would be wise enough to predict the growth industries of the future and to redeploy the nation's economic resources into those areas. Mistakes would be made on a gigantic scale, and the market would not provide much help in rectifying such errors.

The adoption by the Conservative administration of Margaret

Nationalized Companies

Thatcher in Great Britain of an industrial policy that put government financing into selected new industrial areas—such as computers and biogenetics—suggests that the idea of an industrial policy will be very hard to avoid in the United States, no matter who is in power. Some type of industrial policy, whether in the form of planning, or in the form of new financial institutions (like the Reconstruction Finance Corporation), may come into being to help U.S. firms compete in the world and to prevent the demise of many American firms through inadequate long-run financing.

COMMAND CAPITALISM: SCENARIO 4

The previous scenarios assume that the political system of the United States will remain unchanged during the rest of this century. While the possibility exists of change in the structure of our government, through a military coup, or the election of a president who is a demagogue, a more likely scenario of this variety simply suggests a shift to what we might call command capitalism.

Command capitalism is a version of our present system except that the president assumes the role of commander-in-chief of the economy in both peace and war—with all that implies. It can be thought of as equivalent to war-time capitalism. The executive branch of government becomes permanently dominant. This transition has been in progress throughout this century, as president and the bureaucracy have continued to increase in power. Congress, by contrast, is stalemated by conflicting interest groups.

The country has long suffered through interest group stalemate, but the powers of a mediatory presidency have usually been sufficient to effect compromise. As interest groups have become more vigorous and disclosed their positions more forcefully in the media, their leaders have been less able to trade votes and log-roll to make legislation possible. Crises in foreign or domestic affairs require action, and this pressure could force the emergence of a full command presidency. It can be argued that this is already occurring with the powers presently available to the president as commander-in-chief. During war or extraordinary crises, the president's specific and implied command power enables him to cut through traditional restraints. This is precisely the power needed to overcome interest group stalemate in Congress.

What effect would a command presidency have on the economic system? We have only to look at World War II to see the prototype.

The president would direct national economic planning in order to guarantee economic stability at home and to insure that public and private sector programs work harmoniously. Further controls—especially of wages and prices—on a permanent basis seem to be inevitable in such a model. Investment controls and many of the programs advocated by the neo-liberals would be the president's arsenal. If crises became more acute, the command presidency, even if its ostensible purpose was to rescue private enterprise, would intrude more deeply into the private sector.

Just as Rome evolved from the Republic into the Empire under Caesar, there are pressures for the transformation of democracies in crisis to more centralized forms of government—not necessarily through choice, but through expediency.

EUROPEAN DEMOCRATIC SOCIALISM: SCENARIO 5

In this scenario, capitalism gradually withers away, as is happening in Western Europe. Capitalism would not disappear overnight, but increasing nationalization or control of industry and increased planning would slowly eliminate the private sector. The ideology of capitalism—private property, the limited role of government, market entrepreneurship, and the profit motive—would eventually be extinguished. Certainly, the neo-liberals would favor many of the programs that the Europeans have adopted in the last twenty-five years to revitalize their own economies. Protectionism and economic nationalism would become a major feature of any such scenario, as it has in Europe in recent decades.

This scenario has been explained in detail throughout this book as we have shown how nationalization operates in various forms in Europe. However, continued crises—economic, social, and eventually war—might well force the system into a command socialist model.

CONCLUSION

We have looked at a number of alternative scenarios for the future of American capitalism. Despite the possibilities of command capitalism, we remain cautiously optimistic that both democracy and bureaucratic capitalism will survive this century in the United States. We are considerably less sanguine about the prospects for survival

Nationalized Companies

of capitalism in Western Europe. Indeed, capitalism in Western Europe appears to be in serious, perhaps irreversible, decline. The future of capitalism and high economic growth is in the Eastern Asian capitalist nations.

The United States stands at the crossroads, debating how best to cope with the problems of industrial transformation. Unfortunately, the United States in the past has adopted many of its ideas and institutions from Western Europe. If American capitalism is to regain its vigor—indeed, if it is to survive—the model of capitalism in Eastern Asian countries present far more likelihood for success than that of Western Europe.

The scenarios we have discussed above suggest some of the routes that the United States is most likely to follow. Whether they will lead to a dynamic, restructured, growing capitalist society remains to be seen. The one scenario that seems less likely to lead in that direction is pursuing the chimera of growth and efficiency through more and more nationalized firms.

NOTES

Introduction

Notes

1. John Kenneth Galbraith, *The New Industrial State* (Boston: Houghton Mifflin, 1973); "Tasks for the Democratic Left," *The New Republic*, August 15 and 23, 1975.
2. Interview with William W. Wimpisinger, *Challenge*, March-April 1978, pp. 44–53.
3. *Congressional Record*, Proceedings and Debates of the 93rd Congress, first session, Washington, November 7, 1973, Vol. 119, No. 17.
4. Felix G. Rohaytn, "Promoting a Second U.S. Industrial Revolution," *International Herald Tribune* (Paris), February 16, 1981.

Chapter 1

Note

1. Edouard Bonnefous, Senat No. 379, *Sur le controle des entreprises publiques*, (France) 1977.

Other Sources

1. *The Economist*, "The State in the Market," December 30, 1978, pp. 37–58.
2. Holland, Stuart. *The State as Entrepreneur*. London: Weidenfeld and Nicolson, 1972.
3. Holland, Stuart. "Europe's New Public Enterprises," in Raymond Vernon, ed. *Big Business and the State: Changing Relations in Western Europe*. Cambridge: Harvard, 1974.
4. Keutgen, Rene. "The Proposals for the Reorganization of Industrial Assets Owned by the Federal German Government." *Annals of Public and Cooperative Economy*, October–December, 1974, pp. 347–368.
5. Keyser, William, and Ralph Windle, eds. *Public Enterprise in the EEC*. Sijthoff & Noordhoff, 1978.
6. Lacina, Ferdinand. "The Development of the Austrian Public Sector Since World War II," Technical Paper Series No. 7, Institute of Latin American Studies. The University of Texas at Austin, 1977.
7. Lamont, Douglas F. *Foreign State Enterprises*. New York: Basic Books, 1979.
8. Monsen, R. Joseph; and Walters, Kenneth D. "State-Owned Firms: A Review of the Data and Issues," in Lee Preston, ed. *Research in Corporate Social Performance and Policy*, Vol. 2, pp. 125–156. JAI Press, 1980.

9. Saraceno, Pasquale. "The Italian System of State-Held Enterprises." *Journal of International Law and Economics*, Vol. 11, 1977, pp. 407–446.

10. Shepherd, William G. "Public Enterprise in Western Europe and the United States," in de Jong, ed. *The Structure of European Industry*. Martinus Mijhoff, 1981.

11. Stoffaes, Christian; and Victorri, Jacques. *Nationalisations*. Paris: Flammarion, 1977.

12. Tornblom, Lars. "The Swedish State Company Limited: Statsforetag AB: Its Role in the Swedish Economy." *Annals of Public and Cooperative Economy*, October–December, 1977, pp. 451–461.

13. Walters, Kenneth; and Monsen, R. Joseph. "State-Owned Firms Abroad: New Competitive Threat." *Harvard Business Review*, March–April, 1979.

Chapter 2

Notes

1. William Pfaff, "France and Japan: Soul Mates?" *International Herald Tribune* (Paris), May 8, 1981.

2. *Ibid.*

3. "Mitterrand: Why Nationalization Will Work." *The Wall Street Journal*, October 7, 1981.

4. William Pfaff, "Reflections: Elitists and Egalitarians." *The New Yorker*, September 28, 1981.

5. John Redwood, *Public Enterprise in Crisis*. (Oxford: Blackwell, 1980), p. 1.

6. R. H. Tawney, *The Acquisitive Society*, 1920.

Chapter 3

Notes

1. Pierre Dreyfus, *La Liberté de Réussir* (Paris: Jean-Claude Simoën, 1977).

2. Pierre Meutey and Eric Roig, "La Croisade de M. Anti-nationalisations," *Figaro*, September 19, 1981.

3. Anthony King, "Overload: Problems of Governing in the 1970s," *Political Studies*, Vol. 23 (1975), pp. 284–296.

4. W. A. Robson, "Labour's Nationalisation Programme," *Political Quarterly*, Vol. 45, No. 4 (October–December 1974), p. 403.

5. Dudley Jackson, Book Review in *The Economic Journal*, September 1975, pp. 683–685.

6. Franco A. Grassini, "The Italian Enterprises: The Political Constraints," in Raymond Vernon and Yair Aharoni, eds., *State-Owned*

Enterprises in the Western Economies (New York: St. Martin's Press, 1981).

Other Sources

1. "The Economic Policy of the Italian Communist Party Described." *Challenge*, October 1976. p. 35.
2. Coombes, David. *State Enterprise: Business or Politics?* London: George Allen and Unwin, Ltd., 1971.
3. Doz, Yves. "Multinational Strategy and Structure in Government Controlled Businesses." *Columbia Journal of World Business*, Fall 1980, pp. 14–25.
4. Mazzolini, Renato. "Government Controlled Enterprises: What's the Difference?" *Columbia Journal of World Business*, Summer 1980, pp. 28–37.
5. Millward, Robert. "Price Restraint, Anti-Inflation Policy and Public and Private Industry in the United Kingdom 1949–1973." *The Economic Journal*, June 1976, pp. 226–242.
6. Robson, William A. "Mixed Enterprise." *National Westminister Bank Quarterly Review*, August 1972, pp. 22–34.
7. Smith, P. S. "Petrobras: The Politicizing of a State Company, 1953–1964." *Business History Review*, Summer 1972.
8. Vernon, Raymond. "The International Aspects of State-Owned Enterprises." *Journal of International Business Studies*, Winter 1979, pp. 7–15.
9. Vernon, Raymond and Yair Aharoni, eds., *State-Owned Enterprise in the Western Economies* (New York: St. Martin's Press, 1981).
10. Walters, Kenneth and Monsen, R. Joseph, "The Nationalized Firm," *Columbia Journal of World Business*, Spring 1977.

Chapter 4

Notes

1. *The Nora Report* ("Rapport sur les enterprises publiques") (Paris: Documentation Francaise, 1967).
2. Dow Votaw, *The Six-Legged Dog: Mattei and ENI* (Berkeley and Los Angeles: University of California Press, 1964).
3. Pierre Dreyfus, *La Liberté de Réussir* (Paris: Jean-Claude Simoën, 1977).

Other Sources

1. Mazzolini, Renato. *Government Controlled Enterprise* New York: John Wiley, 1979.
2. Monsen, R. Joseph and Walters, Kenneth D. "Managing the Nationalized Company." *California Management Review*, 1983.

Nationalized Companies

3. Posner, M. V. and Woolf, S. J. *Italian Public Enterprise* Cambridge: Harvard University Press, 1967.
4. Shepherd, W. G., et al. *Public Enterprise*. Lexington, Mass.: Lexington Books, 1976.

Chapter 5

Notes

1. *Politics and Markets* (New York: Basic Books, 1977), part V.
2. John Kenneth Galbraith, "The Economic Problems of the Left," *The New Statesman*, February 20, 1976, p. 218.
3. Quoted in Anthony Robinson, "The Poles Look Enviously at Hungary," *Financial Times* (London), November 1, 1980.
4. "Whitehall on the Head-hunting Trail for Board Chairmen," *Financial Times* (London), January 21, 1980.
5. Michael Lipton, "What is Nationalization For?" *Lloyd's Bank Review*, August 1976.
6. Sweden's non-socialist Fälldin government removed politicians from Statsföretag's Board.
7. *The Nora Report* ("Rapport sur les enterprises publiques") (Paris: Documentation Franscaise, 1967).
8. In Germany, the government first receives nominations from the interests represented.
9. Great Britain, National Economic Development Office, *A Study of UK Nationalized Industries*, 1976.
10. Great Britain, Command 7131, *The Nationalized Industries*, April 1978.
11. Peter Brannen, et al. *The Worker Directors* (London: Hutchinson, 1976).

Other Source

1. Great Britain, National Economic Development Office. *A Study of UK Nationalized Industries, Background paper 2: Relationships of Government and Public Enterprise in France, West Germany and Sweden*, 1977.

Chapter 6

Notes

1. *Financial Times*, November 23, 1982, p. 17.
2. Felix Kessler, "French Premier Pressing Program to Cut Aid to Ailing Firms, Tax Capital Gains," *The Wall Street Journal*, May 26, 1978, p. 12.
3. "Joseph Takes Hard Line on BSC;" "Bitter Opposition Attack," *Financial Times* (London), June 27, 1980.

Other Sources

1. Eltis, Walter. "The True Deficits of the Public Corporations." *Lloyd's Bank Review*, January 1979, pp. 1–20.
2. Great Britain, National Economic Development Office. *A Study of UK Nationalized Industries*, 1976.
3. Joris, Michel. "The Renault Regie." *Annals of Public and Cooperative Economy*, July–September, 1977, pp. 307–342.
4. Keyser, William; and Windle, Ralph, eds. *Public Enterprise in the EEC*. Sijthoff and Noordhoff, 1978.
5. Kramer, Jane. "A Reporter in Europe." *The New Yorker*, May 29, 1977.
6. Nove, Alec. *Efficiency Criteria for Nationalized Industries*. London: Allen & Unwin, 1973.
7. Pryke, Richard. *Public Enterprise in Practice*. MacGibbon and Kee, 1971.
8. Pryke, Richard. *The Nationalized Industries: Policies and Performance Since 1968*. Oxford: Martin Robertson, 1981.
9. Shepherd, William G. *Economic Performance under Public Ownership*, 1965.
10. Shepherd, William G. "Public Enterprise in Western Europe and the United States," in H.W. de Jong, ed. *The Structure of European Industry*. Martinus Nijhoff, 1981.

Chapter 7

Notes

1. "Subsidies and Trade," *The Financial Times* (London), November 23, 1977.
2. Melvyn B. Krauss, *The New Protectionism* (New York: New York University Press, 1978).
3. Pasquale Saraceno, "The Italian System of State-Held Enterprises," *Journal of International Law and Economics*, 1977.
4. *The Economist*, Special Report on "The State in the Market," December 30, 1978.
5. M. M. Kostecki, "State Trading," paper presented at a 1979 conference on State-Owned Enterprises at the Harvard Business School, a shortened version of which is published in Raymond Vernon and Yair Aharoni, eds., *State-Owned Enterprise in the Western Economies* (New York: St. Martin's Press, 1981).
6. T. Ozawa, "Japan's New 'Resource Diplomacy,'" *The World Economy*, 1979.
7. *Ibid.*
8. Kostecki, "State Trading."
9. Chalmers Johnson, *Japan's Public Policy Companies* (Washington D.C.

and Stanford, Calif.: American Enterprise Institute and Hoover Institution on War, Revolution and Peace, 1978).
10. *The Economist*, July 29, 1978, p. 89.

Other Sources

1. Aharoni, Yair. "The State Owned Enterprise as a Competitor in International Markets." *Columbia Journal of World Business*, Spring, 1980.
2. Aharoni, Yair. "The Role of the Public Sector in the Face of Economic Crisis." *Annals of Public and Cooperative Economy*, July–December 1976.
3. Cao, A. D. "Non-tariff Barriers to U.S. Manufactured Exports." *Columbia Journal of World Business*, Summer 1980, pp. 93–102.
4. Heenan, David A.; and Keegan, Warren J. "The Rise of Third World Multinationals." *Harvard Business Review*, January–February, 1979.
5. Jacquemin, Alexis. et al. "A Dynamic Analysis of Export Cartels: The Japanese Case." *The Economic Journal*, September, 1981, pp. 685–696.
6. Mathijsen, P. "State Aids, State Monopolies, and Public Enterprise in the Common Market." *Law and Contemporary Problems*, Spring 1972.
7. Mazzolini, Renato. "Are State-Owned Enterprises Unfair Competition?" *California Management Review*, Winter 1980, pp. 20–28.
8. Rukeyser, William S. "Creeping Capitalism in Government Corporations." *Fortune*, September 15, 1968.
9. Vernon, Raymond. "International Economic Relations in Transition." *The World Economy*, March 1981, pp. 17–27.
10. Walters, Kenneth and Monsen, R. Joseph, "State-Owned Firms Ahead: New Competitive Threat." *Harvard Business Review*, July–August 1979.

Chapter 8

Notes

1. Grassini, "Political Constraints," in Vernon and Aharoni, eds., *State-Owned Enterprises*.
2. Robert Bacon and Walter Eltis, "Britain's Economic Problem: The Growth of the Non-Market Sector?" *The Economic Journal*, V. 89 (June, 1979), pp. 392–401; John Redwood, "The Future of the Nationalized Industries," *Lloyd's Bank Review*, April 1976; Michael Lipton, "What is Nationalization For?" *Lloyd's Bank Review*, August 1976; John Redwood, *Public Enterprise in Crisis* (Oxford: Basil Blackwell, 1980); Theodore Geiger, *Welfare and Efficiency* (National Planning Association, 1978).
3. James Q. Wilson, "The Politics of Regulation," in James McKie, ed., *Social Responsibility and the Business Predicament* (Brookings, 1974).
4. Abram Bergson, "The Politics of Socialist Efficiency," *The American Economist*, Fall, 1979.

Chapter 9

Notes

1. M. Moskowvitz, et al. eds., *Everybody's Business: An Almanac* (New York: Harper & Row, 1980), p. 633.
2. Quoted in ibid., p. 595.
3. Ezra F. Vogel, "Meeting the Japanese Challenge," *The Wall Street Journal*, May 19, 1980, editorial page.

Chapter 10

Notes

1. Paul Seabury, "NATO: Thinking About the Unmentionable," *The Wall Street Journal*, December 24, 1981.
2. William G. Shepherd, "Public Enterprise in Western Europe and the United States," in H.W. de Jong, ed., *The Structure of European Industry* (Martinus Nijhoff, 1981).

INDEX

171

172

Nationalized Companies

CGT, 39
Chalandon, Albin, 41, 55
Charbonnages de France, 59, 74, 82, 84, 98, 108, 113
Chemicals, 1, 2–3, 4, 5, 10, 11, 12, 13, 14, 20, 21, 22, 27, 87, 93
and America in export markets, 102
Chemie Linz, 14
Chévènement, Jean-Pierre, 30
Chrysler, 12, 43
bail-out, xi, xii, 6, 95, 134, 138–139, 158
CII-Honeywell Bull, 3
CIT-Alcatel, 2
Citroën, 3, 83, 85, 99
Coal industry, 58, 59, 60–63, 74, 82, 84, 89, 98, 100, 108, 111, 113, 114, 130–131, 150
Cockerill, 82, 84, 150
Command capitalism, 160–161
Communications industry, 10, 122, 148
Compagnie Générale d'Electricité, 38
Companies (see Nationalized)
Competition, international, 25–26, 102–103, 138
(*See also* Competition with private companies)
Competition with private companies, 102–120, 135, 139–140
free trade, 103–105, 110–111
and nationalization, 105–106
protectionist policies, 106–119, 127, 144–145, 148
bankruptcy, no fear of, 112–113
built-in markets, 109–111
hidden subsidies, 119
monopoly power, 111–112, 118, 127–128
preferential financing, 107–109, 114, 117–118, 148
profits not necessary, 106–107
restraining actions, 116–119
subsidization of domestic industry, 113–116
U.S. alternatives, 142–148
U.S. policy options, 119–120
Compower, 100
Computers, xi, 1, 2, 3, 12, 16, 20, 21, 100, 109–110, 125, 143, 146, 150, 160
Comsat, 158
Consolidated Coal, 12
Consumer goods, 151
Contracts, long-term, international, 115–116, 145–146
Contracts, program, 57, 73–74
Control of nationalized companies (*see* Nationalized)
Copeba, 2
Copperweld, xi
Crédit Commercial de France, 38
Credit Italiano, 11
Crédit Lyonnais, 37, 38
Creslenn (Dallas), 12

Cross-subsidization, 114–116
Cyclops Corporation, 102

Dassault, 3, 78, 86, 108
Davignon Plan, 117
Defense, national, 137–138, 140, 141, 142
de Gaulle, Charles; Gaullists, 1, 26, 60
De Michelis, Gianni, 39–40
Democracies, and efficient management, 133
Democratic procedures, 69
Dreyfus, Pierre, 35, 43, 54, 57, 59–60, 62–63
Du Pont, 12
Dutch State Mines, 95, 97

East Asia, new capitalist nations, 153, 155, 159, 162
Economic nationalism, 23–25, 109–110
Economic theory, challenge to, 101
Economist, The, 17, 119
Edison, Thomas A., 156
Edwards, Michael, 46, 56, 125
EEC (*see* European Economic Community)
Efficiency and welfare, 130–133
(*See also* Nationalization)
EGAM (Italian holding company), 9
Egidi, Egidio, 41
El Al, 50
Electricité de France, 74
Electricity; electronic equipment, xi, 1, 2, 3, 5, 9, 10, 13, 17, 20, 21, 41, 114, 119, 130, 143, 150
Electricity Board (British), 61
Electricity Council (British), 75
Elf-Aquitaine, 4–5, 41, 55, 66, 95, 97, 100
Elliott, John, 72
Employee/sales ratio, 88, 92, 96
Employment maintenance, 27, 48, 53, 104, 107, 111, 113, 132, 135, 139
England (*see* Great Britain)
ENI (Italian holding company), 9, 10, 39–40, 41, 57, 58–59, 66, 81, 92, 97, 116, 149
Entreprise Minière et Chimique, 95
Ericsson, 114
Europe, decline of, 152–154
European Commission (*see* European Economic Community)
European Economic Community (EEC), 26, 102–103, 112, 116–118, 119
Eximbank (*see* United States Export-Import Bank)
Export-Import Bank of Japan, 115, 116
Exports, maintaining, 104, 107, 131
(*See also* International competition)
Extractive industries, 151
Ezra, Derek, 58, 60–63, 64

Fabian socialism, 32–33
Failing companies, rescuing, xii, 6, 27, 53, 132, 137–140, 147, 149
Fälldin government (Sweden), 135
Federal German Government (*see* West Germany)

Nationalized Companies